"In the silence between worlds, echoes the power of the Universe, where destiny whispers and paths converge"

Voice of the Portals I

THE FIRST GATEWAY

HELLEVI E. WOODMAN

"Voice of The Portals I: The First Gateway"

Copyright © 2024 by Hellevi E. Woodman
All rights reserved.

No part of this publication may be reproduced, distributed, or transmitted in any form or by any means, including photocopying, recording, or other electronic or mechanical methods, without the prior written permission of the publisher, except for brief quotations embodied in critical reviews and specific other noncommercial uses permitted by copyright law. For more information about the book, the author, or related resources, please contact: hellevie@hotmail.com

Printed in the United States of America First Edition, 2024

Library of Congress Control Number: 2024907705
ISBN: 979-8-9905095-0-4 (e-book)
ISBN: 979-8-9905095-1-1 (Paperback)

Published by Hellevi E. Woodman Ft Lauderdale, Florida

Disclaimer:

This book, "Voice of the Portals I, The First Gateway "including all content, insights, practices, and stories, is intended for informational and inspirational purposes only. The views and experiences shared by the author reflect personal journeys and explorations and are not intended as medical, legal, or professional advice. The author and publisher disclaim any liability directly or indirectly for using the material in this book.

While the practices and rituals described have benefited the author and others, they may not produce the same results for everyone. Readers are encouraged to approach these practices with an open mind and adapt them according to their beliefs, circumstances, and needs.

The author and publisher have made every effort to ensure the accuracy of the information within this book was correct at press time. However, the author and publisher do not assume and hereby disclaim any liability to any party for any loss, damage, or disruption caused by errors or omissions, whether such errors or omissions result from negligence, accident, or any other cause.

Readers are responsible for their well-being and must take personal responsibility for using any practices or insights in this book. It is always recommended to consult with a professional healthcare provider before starting any new health-related practice or if you have any concerns about your mental or physical health. The stories and examples herein are shared to inspire and engage; they are invitations to explore the depths of your journey, not prescriptions or directives. Remember, you are your most insightful guide on the path to personal growth and understanding.

DEDICATION

To the unseen guides and whispering spirits of the Earth, whose silent voices have guided me through the veils of reality and into the heart of the mystical.

To the ancient guardians of wisdom, the animals, the trees, the stones, the mountains, and the waters, for sharing their timeless stories and sacred energies with an open heart.

This book is dedicated to you, the dreamers, seekers, explorers, and wanderers who walk the delicate line between worlds, searching for the magic hidden in plain sight.

To those who find profound joy in the quiet of dawn, who see the stories woven in the wind, and who hear the whispers of the earth in the rustle of leaves—this journey is for you.

To my family, friends, and teachers whose unwavering support and love have been my anchor and wings, this journey is as much yours as it is mine.

And to the Earth, our beautiful, living home, which teaches us daily about resilience, beauty, and the intricate dance of life—thank you for your endless inspiration and for holding us all in your embrace.

May this book be a gateway to new worlds within and without, inspiring you to discover the portals of wonder that await in the every day and the extraordinary. May we all walk gently, love deeply, and live magically.

TABLE OF CONTENTS

Preface: Gateway to the Mystical 13

Introduction: The Journey Begins 15

Chapter I: Sacred Landscapes and Energies 19
  "A Tear in the Fabric of Time"—Peru 21
  "Spiraling into Existence"—Easter Island 24
  "Cosmic Waters"—New Zealand 26
  "A Sensory Odyssey"—New Zealand 30
Reflections and Practices: Linking the Sacred and Everyday ... 32
My Path to Connection: Practices I Cherish 35
  Grounding: Earth's Embrace 35
  Mindfulness Amidst the Wild: Nature's Whisper 36
  The Impact of Wonder: Awe's Echo 37
  The Art of Journaling: Soulful Reflections 38

Chapter II: Journeys of Transformation 41
  "The Initiation Well"—Portugal 43
  "The Journey of the Wounded Healers"—Peru 45
  "A Heroic Journey"—New Zealand 48
Reflections and Practices: Embracing Change 50

Inner Transformation: My Rituals of Change 52
One Breath at a Time 53
Creating Personal Rituals of Transformation 54
Crafting My Epic 55

Chapter III: Encounters with the Unseen 59
"Playing in the Cosmic Symphony"—Portugal 61
"Stillness"—Rapa Nui 63
"Awaken Dreamwalkers"—Australia 67
"Interstellar Capitol"—Washington D.C. 70
Reflections and Practices: Beyond the Veil 72
Connecting to the Unseen: My Pathway to Mystery 74
Inner Journeys 74
Dreamscape Chronicles 75
My Inner Sanctum: Personal Check-Ins 76

Chapter IV: Guardians of Wisdom and Laughter 79
"Mystical Realms"—New Zealand 80
"Settle in the Stones"—New Zealand 83
"Whispers of the Wild"—New Zealand 85
"Namaskar Cucaracha"—Rapa Nui 88
Reflections and Practices: The Lighter Side of Spirit 91
Wisdom and Laughter: Playing Life Grand Games 92
Joyful Groove: Dance as Therapy 92
Colorful Expressions: Releasing our Inner Artist 93

A Heartfelt Connection: Hug a Tree *94*
Laughter Therapy: Hasna Yoga *94*

Chapter V: Cycles of Nature and Life 97
"Paradox of Existence"—Australia *98*
"Day of the Dead"—Mexico *101*
"Final Savasana"—Asana Practice *103*
Reflections and Practices: The Eternal Dance 106
Embracing Nature's Cycles: Blending Daily Intentions with Personal Rituals 108
Lunar Alchemy: Fire & Moon Ceremonies *108*
Sacred Space: Altar Creation *110*
The Gateway to Living Fully: Mindfulness of Death *111*
Simply Grateful: Gratitude Practice *112*

Epilogue: Beyond the First Gateway 115

Acknowledgments 119

Journey to the Heart 123

Glossary of Terms 125

Further Readings 129

About Me 133

PREFACE

GATEWAY TO THE MYSTICAL

As I sit down to write "Voice of the Portals I: The First Gateway," it feels less like beginning a new project and more like opening a cherished diary, one filled with tales of adventure, moments of stillness, and countless lessons learned along the way.

This book, woven from the threads of my travels and the quiet moments in between, is a deeply personal narrative that bridges our planet's vast and mystical landscapes with the seemingly small yet profoundly sacred experiences that shape our existence.

Each chapter and story within these pages springs from my heart, crafted from my moments of awe in the presence of ancient wonders and from those instances of unexpected clarity that often arrive during the simplest of daily activities.

From the awe-inspiring peaks of Machu Picchu, where the past whispers to the present, to the silent, starlit nights on Easter Island that speak of deep mysteries, and the green, healing lands of New Zealand, each place has gifted me stories of connection, not just with the land but with the essence of what it means to be human.

However, this journey is not only about the destinations that dot the map; it is also about those moments that might seem inconsequential at first glance—a shared laugh with friends that brings a deep sense of belonging, a quiet morning that reminds us of the beauty of simply being, or the profound peace found in a mindful moment that is fully present. These, too, are portals to discover, each teaching us about the beauty of life in its myriad forms.

This book is my invitation to you—not just to read about my experiences but to join me in recognizing the extraordinary in the ordinary, to find those portals of transformation in your own life, whether at ancient sites or in the comfort of your home.

As you turn these pages, I hope you will see reflections of your journey, finding resonance and inspiration to seek out the magic hidden in plain sight.

Welcome to the first gateway, where each step forward invites us to unveil the marvels that lie beyond the horizon and deep within ourselves.

INTRODUCTION

THE JOURNEY BEGINS

As I started envisioning "Voice of the Portals I: The First Gateway," I remembered my years of traversing the globe on cruise ships. This odyssey expanded my world's horizons and eventually deepened my journey.

From the earliest days of my childhood, curiosity has been my guiding star. It led me from the mystical whispers of trees and animals in my backyard to the stages of cruise ships, sailing to lands that were once dreams and names on a map.

After traveling to more than 90 countries, I have personally experienced how each landscape has its unique energy, ranging from the bustling streets of cosmopolitan cities to the peaceful environment of untouched nature.

In the last five years, however, I have found myself experiencing a more profound connection with the world within and around me. This inward journey began by questioning my beliefs and life purpose, which led to a transformative shift in how I perceive, experience, and engage with my surroundings.

"Voice of the Portals I: The First Gateway" is a narrative of this recent journey. I would like to invite you to voyage alongside me to mystical sites and into the sacredness of ordinary moments and to feel how these experiences reflect and facilitate our personal growth.

The stories shared here are portals, gateways to understanding the interconnectedness of all things, the deep wisdom held on the land, and the lessons we can draw from being truly present and engaged with the world around us.

Reflecting on my time at sea—navigating both serene and turbulent waters—I have come to embrace the diversity of life and the underlying unity of our human experience. This book weaves my reflections, practices, and some scientific facts to enrich your journey.

I warmly invite you to look within and understand that you are both the portal and the guide on your path. You are the creator and custodian of your journey, equipped with the innate ability to navigate life's mysteries.

As you turn the pages of The First Gateway, let it mirror a quest across the seas and your journey toward profound transformation and discovery.

May you be inspired to explore both the vast world around you and the uncharted territories within your soul.

THE JOURNEY BEGINS

Bon voyage, dear travelers. We are on this adventure together as authors and readers, as fellow travelers on this incredible journey called life.

CHAPTER 1

SACRED LANDSCAPES AND ENERGIES

"Look at this life—all mystery and magic."
— Harry Houdini

Reflecting on these journeys, where the majestic horizons of Machu Picchu, the soul-stirring tranquility of New Zealand, and the enigmatic silhouettes of Easter Island's Moai have each, in turn, whispered the Earth's ancient tales to me, I have come to understand the profound bond we share with these sacred landscapes. These experiences, far removed from our daily lives, have deepened my connection with nature and served as a mirror, reflecting my inner journey toward a deeper understanding and peace.

This chapter is an ode to these moments of connection. It is not just about recounting visits to these extraordinary places but also about sharing the essence of what they represent—the potent, raw energies that these sites emanate and how they resonate with our energies.

With their profound spiritual significance, these sacred spaces have the power to recalibrate our essence, aligning us closely with the rhythm of the natural world.

As I can recall, I was in awe, standing amidst the remnants of Machu Picchu. This was a civilization that harmoniously blended with its environment, a testament to the sacred balance between humanity and nature.

New Zealand, with its verdant landscapes and robust cultural heritage, taught me about the deep respect and reverence for land that is central to Māori culture.

Easter Island, a place shrouded in mystery, offered lessons on resilience, laughter, and the importance of understanding our place within the larger narrative of the world.

This chapter invites you to see beyond the physical beauty of these places and feel the Earth's pulse beneath your feet. It is also a call to recognize the sacredness surrounding us, often unnoticed, in our everyday lives.

Through these stories, I hope to inspire a reconnection with the natural world, an appreciation for its wisdom, and a realization that searching for magic and meaning is a journey through the external world and the uncharted territories of our inner being.

"A Tear in the Fabric of Time"—Peru

In the summer of 2023, I embarked on a pilgrimage with a small group of medicine women in training, setting the stage for a transformative journey unlike any I had experienced before. Our destination was Machu Pichu, a place shrouded in mystery and ancient wisdom. Among the ruins of this sacred place, I hoped to find a deeper connection to the Earth's sacred sites and their energies.

The physical challenges of the journey, the steep ascent through the Andes, and the weariness in my limbs all faded into insignificance in the face of this profound certainty that I have walked these paths before, that I have stood in this very spot in another lifetime.

This made the entire experience feel like a déjà vu that defied explanation. It was as if time had folded back on me, and I was a traveler in space and the realms of history and memory.

Stepping onto the ancient citadel, the sensation of being watched, of unseen eyes following my every move, enveloped me. It was an uncanny feeling that defied logic and reason, yet it coursed through my being with eerie familiarity. It was as though the spirits of this sacred place were walking beside me, whispering their secrets to my soul.

As I paused to inhale the crisp mountain air, I was surrounded by a stunning view. The Andes' towering peaks stood guard, their ancient faces bearing witness to generations of humanity. The sky above was a deep shade of blue, almost celestial in its beauty. The sheer magnitude of this place and the breathtaking beauty of nature humbled me to my core.

As I closed my eyes, I suddenly felt a surge of energy. It was like a vortex emanating from the heart of Machu Picchu and surrounding me, moving clockwise in all directions. It felt as if the spirits of this place were inviting me to join them in their eternal dance and become one with the pulsating heartbeat of the Earth.

At that moment, I felt I was at the merging point of two colossal energy pyramids that extended toward the sky and deep into the Earth. I was a humble witness to their power at their intersection between the upper world and inner Earth.

When I opened my eyes, the world around me seemed transformed. The once silent mountains came alive with a new meaning as if they were sacred texts with stories etched into their very being. Symbols, codes, and intricate geometry appeared before me, speaking of a civilization that understood the language of the earth and people who communed with the spirits of the land. Each stone, ridge, and crevice told a tale, a narrative woven into the very fabric of this sacred place.

Standing before a gnarled tree, I noticed its roots intertwined with ancient stones. I placed my hand on its rough bark and connected to the earth's heartbeat beneath my fingertips. The tree had been standing here for centuries, witnessing the rise and fall of civilizations. Now, it shared its wisdom with me.

I explored the citadel, guided not by a map but by an inner compass. Every step, every stone I touched, was a communion with history and spirit. The air was imbued with palpable energy as if the molecules vibrated with a timeless resonance. This was a living library.

As I wandered amidst the towering stone citadel, I discovered more than the ruins of a long-lost civilization; I found a living testament to the sacredness of existence itself. More than a physical trek, this journey was a step through an open portal into a deeper understanding of my human experience, reminding me of the magic that exists around and within. It was a tear in the fabric of time, granting me a glimpse into the eternal and the enduring power of the human spirit.

The day passed in a blur, yet each moment was perfectly etched into my memory. The sun rose and set over the ruins, painting the ancient stones with hues of gold and orange. I sat in meditation with my gaze fixed on the horizon, and in those quiet moments, I felt a deep sense of peace, infinite expansion, and a profound connection to the universe.

As all journeys must, mine came to an end. Descending from Machu Picchu, the physical world asserted itself once more, but I carried a heart brimming with gratitude. The magic of this place lives on, not just in stones and stories but deep within me.

"Spiraling into Existence"—*Easter Island*

In October of 2023, alongside a close-knit sisterhood of fellow medicine women, I ventured to the enigmatic Easter Island. This pilgrimage was not merely a journey across oceans but a dive into the depths of the soul, seeking to uncover truths woven into the fabric of this ancient land.

As we drew closer to Te Pito Kura, I felt a powerful energy all around me. The mystical power that filled this place was palpable, and I could sense it in every fiber of my being. Here, it seemed as though time itself had come to a standstill.

Everything and nothing existed in perfect harmony, creating a void where all dualities and extremes dissolved into a seamless unity. This was where the game of opposites seemed to fade away, leaving only a sense of oneness and tranquility.

Drawn to a stone radiating mysterious energy, I was urged to sit and reflect beside it. In this contemplative state, the distinction between the self and the surroundings blurred, and I pondered the nature of existence in a realm with no polarities. The vast and imposing Pacific Ocean served as the perfect backdrop for this introspection, its waves crashing against the shore echoing the depths of my thoughts. Is the game over when you go beyond duality?

As I was sitting there, I felt a gentle movement in the ground beneath me, which made me question its stability. I wondered if it was an earthquake, but it did not feel like a typical seismic tremor. It was more like a spiraling force that appeared to be emanating from deep within the earth. It felt like the earth's very core was pulsating with unseen electrical forces.

The interplay of magnetic forces and the physical world creates a complex dance that often goes unnoticed. As I stood there, I felt the eternal internal waters moving in a spiral motion, like an unseen river beneath the surface. It felt like an invisible umbilical cord connected me to the earth's womb, serving as a lifeline that linked me to everything above and below.

In that moment, I experienced a tangible connection to the sacred energies and felt like a part of something much greater than myself.

In the presence of Te Pito Kura, my consciousness melded with the ancient vibrancy of the land. The stone beside me whispered stories of old sorrows, inviting me into a dialogue with the island's spirit. Surrounded by the ocean's vastness, I saw my reflections in its depths, engaging in a soulful journey of discovery.

In this mystical experience, I realized that Te Pito Kura is a sacred portal to a reality where the tangible and intangible converge.

The ocean, the stones, and the unseen forces beneath the surface create a space where the veil between the physical and the metaphysical is lifted. This was a powerful reminder that the Earth itself is a living, breathing entity, and within its embrace, I found a profound connection to the mysteries constantly spiraling into existence.

"Cosmic Waters"—New Zealand

In December 2023, my husband and I traveled to New Zealand. We went to the heart of South Island, Aotearoa, fascinated by the stories of its mystical landscapes and ancient waters.

Our adventure unfolded like a sacred Māori narrative, with each location being a chapter in a story woven from the fabric of the earth itself.

We started our journey at Lake Tekapo, nestled by the Southern Alps. The water was crystal clear and shimmered with the brilliance of liquid sapphires. In answering an unspoken call, we embraced the chill of the glacier-fed lake, an immersion that melded the essence of this sacred place with our beings.

A chill ran down my spine when I touched the cold waters of Lake Tekapo. As I drank the pure water, it felt like the essence of the glacier lake merged with every cell in my body, creating a harmonious symphony.

Each drop of water seemed to hold a story of whales, mermaids, and hidden doorways between worlds. The ripples on the water's surface danced with these tales, revealing the secrets beneath them.

The lake became a sacred communion, and I was submerged in the moment. I felt a profound connection to the land's pristine heartbeat and a deep understanding that my experiences constantly echo the resonance of my being.

Our journey followed the curved path of the Haast River. The river appeared as blue veins of the earth carrying cosmic DNA for all life. I sat by its banks and listened to the river's murmurs. Its eloquent language spoke of the unchanging nature of pure water, which reflects our innate selves.

The river became a cosmic storyteller, narrating tales etched in liquid whispers. It provided a timeless narrative of interconnectedness and the eternal flow of life.

As we stood at the shoreline of Lake Wanaka, I felt a sudden and irresistible urge. The rhythmic clapping of the lake's waves against the shore called out to me, and in a moment of pure connection, I felt compelled to sing. With the sun casting a warm glow upon the water, I offered my voice to the lake as a gesture of reciprocity between my spirit and the elemental essence that danced before me.

At our next stop, we witnessed the powerful Devil's Punchbowl waterfall and its symphony in full crescendo. The running waters thundered with a rhythmic heartbeat that echoed the cosmic blueprint flowing within every drop.

The surroundings were veiled in a cold mist, and I extended my hands to feel the pulsating energy. At that moment, I stood not merely before a natural wonder but within the embrace of an energetic force that transcended the boundaries of my ordinary existence.

Upon arriving at Rotorua, the air thickened with pungent sulfur smells, signaling the presence of volcanic springs. As we got closer, the earthy aroma engulfed me, and the warm embrace of the sulfuric waters beckoned unto me. Like alchemical cauldrons, the springs stirred an essence that transcended the tangible. When I dipped my fingers in the springs, I felt the pulse of creation, a potent reminder that the alchemy of earthly and divine forces also lay within the pungency.

Our journey extended to the majestic Pacific Ocean, where the horizon appeared to never end. With each crashing wave, I sensed the ancient tales carried by the ocean currents— the whispers of distant lands and forgotten civilizations. The Pacific became a conduit to the depths of time, an aqueous library where the narratives of countless epochs lay hidden beneath the waves.

The symphony of our journey took an unexpected turn on the shores of Waiheke Island's Blackpool beach. Instead of the vibrant dance of life, we encountered overwhelming algae blooms.

Usually adorned in natural beauty, the beach wore a sinister tone. The air was heavy with an unsettling scent, reminding us of the delicate balance that nature holds. Despite the apparent unwholesomeness, there was a strange beauty in the algae's patterns, a paradoxical dance between life and death.

As our journey ended, a powerful hailstorm arose, and the waters said goodbye with a celestial spectacle. Hailstones were falling from the sky, each carrying the whispers of the storm's spirit.

Amid nature's fury, I stood still, feeling the frozen connection with the elements. In the heart of the storm, I found a sense of surrender to the unpredictable. I became a silent witness to the whimsical beauty that defines the dance between the earth and the sky.

As the sun set, we stood amidst the rejuvenated landscapes and watched a radiant rainbow arch across the sky, becoming the final stroke in nature's masterpiece.

As we left, I carried a sense of the flowing amusement woven by Aotearoa's waters. From glacier lakes to river murmurs and sulfuric springs to powerful waterfalls, the majestic Pacific, and even an unexpected encounter with toxic algae blooms, each form of water granted me a glimpse into the inherent energy of all things.

The waters of Aotearoa are carriers of ancient tales and cosmic truths, and they have become a liquid tapestry where the ordinary and the extraordinary weave in a dance of timeless wonders.

VOICE OF THE PORTALS I: THE FIRST GATEWAY

"A Sensory Odyssey"—New Zealand

The next leg of our journey exploring the wild landscapes of Aotearoa was a truly immersive experience. Surrounded by lush green mountains and the sweet fragrance of native flora carried by the gentle breeze, I felt like I was truly part of this beautiful land. The adventure promised a sensory feast, and I could not wait to explore everything this place had to offer.

Having felt a deep inner calling, I decided to immerse myself again in Aotearoa's shimmering glacier waters. As the cool liquid enveloped me, a surge of vitality flowed through every cell of my body. It was as if the sacred touch of the liquid crystals had orchestrated a symphony of rejuvenation within me. I felt anointed and activated in this watery sanctuary, a perfect fusion of my body and the natural world.

As I stood amid the glacial waters, the land extended an invitation, urging me to capture mental snapshots of the kaleidoscope of emotions it stirred within me.

The sensation of the icy water against my skin became a tangible memory, a moment etched in all layers of my consciousness. It encouraged me not just to witness but to fully immerse myself in the experience of the landscape—to feel it with the depths of my soul, not just with my eyes.

The land whispered its invitation, tempting me to indulge in the rich tapestry of sensory experiences. I felt its essence intermingling with my being as I breathed in the crisp mountain air. The symphony of nature unfolded around me, from the distant rush of waterfalls to the gentle rustle of leaves, inviting me to attune my hearing to the heartbeat of this sacred terrain.

I reached out my fingertips to feel the textures of the earth, sensing the rugged terrain beneath my palms and soles. The land embraced me, and I responded by consciously becoming a part of its intricate mosaic while I tasted its sweet saltiness. This was not just a physical interaction but an exchange of energies that transcended the boundaries between myself and my surroundings.

The air was filled with nature's captivating scent, enticing me to take deep breaths. The fragrance of the mountain flowers, the refreshing aroma of pine, the sweet scent of lupines, and the subtle hints of moss all create a sensory experience. Each breath felt like a connection with the aromatic poetry of the land, a moment of communion with the natural world.

I answered the call to fully experience and savor each moment in this sensory journey. Whether it was the pure, crisp taste of glacier waters, the sweet and delicious nectar of bees, or the lingering aroma of mountain herbs in the air, I was participating in a spiritual ritual that engaged all my senses.

The abundance of flavors this land offers unfolded before me. I took the time to appreciate every nuance, allowing it to become a part of the sensory narrative that defined this extraordinary experience.

As I responded to the land's invitation to engage all my senses, I realized that my experience was not just an act of observation. It was a profound merger of myself and the environment. I was not just witnessing the beauty around me; I was an integral part of it.

I felt like a co-creator in the grand tapestry of this mystical landscape. Once a mere element, the luminous glacier waters became a catalyst for an extra-sensory odyssey. It was a journey that I could revisit at will, where every touch, scent, sound, sight, and taste became another page in the sacred fable of my communion with the enchanting spirits of this planet.

I left with the curiosity of a child, filled with joy, gratitude, and amusement. My soul was immersed in the mystical essence of Aotearoa.

Reflections and Practices:
Linking the Sacred and Everyday

Through my travels to sacred sites like Machu Picchu, Easter Island, and the heart of Aotearoa-New Zealand, I have discovered a profound truth: the sacredness of our planet mirrors the sacredness within ourselves.

Standing in the shadow of Machu Picchu's ancient stones, I was struck by a deeper revelation of connection and continuity, feeling as though time had folded upon itself and allowed me to glimpse into the lives of those who walked these paths before me. It was a moment of clarity where I felt a part of something far greater than myself, a thread in the tapestry of human existence.

The silent guardians of Easter Island, the Moai, taught me about resilience, memory, laughter, and the indelible spirit of humanity. These towering figures, set against the backdrop of an endless ocean, spoke of a community's strength and vulnerability. Here, I felt the Earth's pulse and pondered the legacy we leave behind, the stories etched not just in stone but in the hearts we touch and the Earth we walk.

Diving into the crystal-clear waters of New Zealand, where the Māori traditions speak of the sacred bond between the heavens and earth, I found a reflection of my journey. This reminded me of all life's interconnectedness, the delicate balance that sustains us, and the cosmic tapestry to which we all belong.

These experiences are not just markers of my physical journey across our planet but signposts of an inward journey we can undertake.

Reflecting on these sacred landscapes, I understand that our encounters with them are not passive; they are dialogues, energy exchanges, and wisdom exchanges if we are open to listening and receiving.

I have realized that the concept of sacredness is not something distant or separate from my daily life. Rather, it is intimately connected to the everyday moments of my existence. I have discovered the sacred in the laughter shared with friends, in completing my daily chores, in the peace and beauty of a quiet morning, in my ability to stay strong in the face of challenges, and in the eyes of strangers.

I invite you to explore the sacred spaces within your own life. These places do not have to be marked on any map; they are the spaces where you feel alive and more like yourself. They can be as grand as a mountain peak or as humble as your backyard at dawn.

The journey toward recognizing these spaces invites us to see the world and ourselves through a lens of wonder and interconnectedness.

Reflective Questions:

- Can you reflect on a natural landscape that holds special significance for you? What memories or feelings does it evoke? Consider visiting this place again with the intention of connecting on a deeper level. If a visit is not possible, try to recreate the essence of this place in a quiet corner of your home. Spend some time there each day, meditating on your connection to the land and the lessons it offers.
- What elements of your chosen landscape resonate most deeply with you?

- How does this landscape influence your feelings of connectedness to the earth and the broader universe?

Remember, our journey through life is rich with external and internal landscapes. Each one offers unique lessons and insights, guiding us toward a deeper understanding of our place in the universe. Embrace these sacred spaces, for they are not only sanctuaries of beauty and peace but also teachers of profound wisdom.

My Path to Connection: Practices I Cherish

In my journey of self-discovery and connection with the natural world, I have found joy and solace in practices that ground me, enhance my mindfulness, and encourage reflection.

Sharing these practices is about offering tools and inviting you into parts of my daily rhythm that have profoundly shifted how I perceive and engage with the world around me.

Grounding: Earth's Embrace:

I step outside barefoot each morning to greet the earth. This ritual connects me to the planet's energy, and I imagine roots extending from my feet into the depths below.

This practice acknowledges my intertwined existence with the earth, a silent conversation with the soil and spirit of the place I call home.

My morning ritual of connecting with the earth barefoot is inspired by the practice known as "Grounding" or "Earthing." Research has shown that this simple act offers numerous health benefits, including reducing inflammation, improving sleep quality, decreasing stress levels, and enhancing overall well-being. When our skin makes direct contact with the earth, we absorb its electrons, which are powerful natural antioxidants.

This practice is more than just a routine; it is a profound connection with the earth, an energetic embrace that rejuvenates and nourishes my day from the outset.

Mindfulness Amidst the Wild: Nature's Whisper:

My walks in nature are never just walks. They are pilgrimages to the heart of life itself. I pause to truly observe the shades of green, listen to sounds, smell the flowers, or feel the intricate patterns of a single stone.

These moments of deep observation are my lessons in presence, teaching me the language of the natural world, a dialect of colors, textures, flavors, smells, sounds, and silences. The transformative power of nature on the human spirit is well-documented. Spending time in nature significantly reduces cortisol levels and improves mood. My walks embody what scientists call "Nature Mindfulness," a practice that combines mindfulness with environmental immersion, enhancing emotional well-being and a profound sense of connectedness.

This practice amplifies my sensory experiences and connects me to nature's restorative power, aligning with scientific understanding.

The Impact of Wonder: Awe's Echo:

I intentionally look for experiences that inspire a sense of wonder within me. I observe the beauty of nature, letting my gaze roam gently and calmly, which helps me relax my nervous system and feel a deep sense of connection beyond my thoughts.

Incorporating the awe effect into my practices, especially during nature walks, enhances my overall well-being. Whether marveling at the intricate design of a leaf, the vastness of the sky, art, or the complex beauty of a landscape, these moments of awe become powerful tools for grounding and healing. They remind me of the beauty and interconnectedness of all things, reinforcing the importance of presence and mindfulness in my daily life.

Moments of awe can lead to significant shifts in our perspective, making our worries and stresses seem smaller by comparison. Scientifically, research demonstrates how experiences of awe can lead to increased feelings of connectedness, improved mood, and even decreased inflammatory markers in the body.

The Art of Journaling: Soulful Reflections:

Each night, I turn to my journal to weave the tapestry of my day, threading moments of connection, insights or the wisdom gained from challenges.

My journal is a sacred space, a container of my dialogue with life, a record of the small yet significant encounters that mark my path. Journaling, a daily ritual for me, is a conduit for reflection and integration.

By transcribing the day's experiences, emotions, and insights onto paper, I am engaging in a process that psychologists have found to be a powerful tool for self-exploration and emotional processing. This practice is a mirror and a compass, guiding me toward greater self-awareness and understanding.

Incorporating these scientifically proven practices into my daily routine made me find myself at the intersection of ancient wisdom and modern knowledge. These rituals serve as personal anchors and universal paths to well-being, supported by research and enriched by experience.

As I pause at the threshold between the sacred landscapes and the transformative journeys that await, I find myself reflecting on the deep connection between the energy of the places I have visited and the personal metamorphosis that emerges on the horizon.

The sacred sites, with their ancient whispers and vibrant energies, have laid the groundwork for a deeper exploration into the essence of transformation. They have shown me that each stone, tree, and ripple of water carries within it stories of change and renewal.

Standing here, at the cusp of new discoveries, I carry forward the lessons of the earth's eternal dance, ready to delve into the personal transformations that mirror the natural world's ceaseless evolution.

The journey ahead promises not just a change of scenery but a profound shift within, beckoning me to embrace the unknown with an open heart and a curious spirit.

CHAPTER II

JOURNEYS OF TRANSFORMATION

"Just when the caterpillar thought the world was over, it became a butterfly"—Unknown.

The passing of time is marked by the gentle rhythm of the moon's waxing and waning. Similarly, our lives undergo cycles of transformation that challenge us, shape us, and ultimately redefine who we are. This chapter invites us to take the path less traveled, embrace the unknown, and discover what lies beyond the familiar terrains of our existence.

In recent years, I have consciously tried to step out of my comfort zone. I have found that in these moments of discomfort, when faced with challenges and vulnerabilities, I am presented with the greatest opportunities for personal growth.

By venturing outside of what is familiar to me, I can

delve deeper into my psyche and embark on a journey of self-discovery, exploring the intricate landscapes of my soul.

From the mystical depths of the Initiation Well in Sintra, Portugal, where the spiral staircase descends into the earth, inviting us to explore the depths of our subconscious, to the rugged trails of the Salkantay Trek in Peru, which tests our physical limits and resilience, every story in this chapter is a testament to the transformative power of embracing the physical journey as a conduit to inner discovery.

Embarking on a journey across Aotearoa-New Zealand, where the Māori culture weaves a rich tapestry of connection between the land and its people, I was reminded of the heroic journeys we all undertake. It is a land where the stories of ancestors and the natural world come together, teaching us about strength, resilience, and the interconnectedness of all life.

"Journeys of Transformation" is about the places we visit and what happens to us along the way. It is about the moments of clarity that come when we push ourselves beyond our limits, the profound connections we forge with others, and the deep sense of belonging we find in the most unexpected places.

This chapter is a pilgrimage through the landscapes of our souls, inviting you to explore the treasure in challenges that have the power to transform us.

As we journey together through these pages, I hope you find reflections of your transformative journeys and feel inspired to step out of your comfort zone and embrace the cycles of transformation that lead us to discover who we truly are.

"The Initiation Well"—Portugal

During my first pilgrimage with the Medicine Woman's School in October 2022, I had an incredible experience that took me to the heart of Sintra, Portugal. I found myself in Quinta da Regaleira, an estate where reality and fantasy seamlessly blend. As soon as I crossed the entrance, I felt like I had stepped into a storybook, where the air was filled with magic, and every corner promised to reveal hidden secrets.

As I wandered through the garden, I suddenly realized I had been separated from my fellow sisters. I felt a soft panic rising within me, and my mind began to call forth worst-case scenarios. Amidst the inner chaos, a gentle whisper asked me: "Can you trust enough to walk the path with your eyes closed?" With only my inner compass to follow, it felt like a challenge from the universe itself.

With determination, I closed my eyes and began my sensory journey. The cool, slightly uneven ground beneath my bare feet hinted at the hidden wonders ahead. The symphony of rustling leaves and distant bird songs guided me, replacing my fear with a growing sense of connection on this path of synchronistic revelations.

Navigating through this mystical maze, I felt an extraordinary expansion of my energy field with each step. It was as if the very essence of the place was infusing me with newfound vitality.

Once a reserved passage for a select few on their initiatory paths, the Initiation Well now calls to all who seek a deeper connection and an awakening of their dormant initiate within.

As I moved through the spiraling depths of the well, I pondered a question. Are we all revisiting our footprints in some way? The air was thick with ancient energies, and it seemed to trigger dormant memories to awaken within me. I felt like I was joining an ethereal dance between the past and present.

As I continued my journey, I could not help but find humor in the absurdity of my initial panic. It seemed like the universe and my guides had a mischievous sense of humor, constantly challenging me to trust in the unseen and embrace the unknown while paying close attention. With a chuckle, I realized that sometimes, getting lost is the first step to finding oneself.

I learned that trust is not just an external reliance but an inner compass that guides us through life's twists and turns. Closing my eyes metaphorically reminded me to trust my instincts, even when the path seemed uncertain.

Quinta da Regaleira, with its Initiation Well, became a metaphor for life's journey—a magical, sometimes challenging, but ultimately transformative adventure. It reminded me that we are all initiates in the grand tapestry of existence, each step unraveling the mysteries of our consciousness.

Leaving this enchanted realm, I carried with me the

memories of a fairy-tale-like experience and the taste of absolute trust in my inner guidance as I embraced the unknown.

Quinta da Regaleira had not only opened its gates to my physical presence but had initiated a profound awakening within—a reminder that, in this mystical journey of life, we are all revisiting our path of magic and self-discovery.

"The Journey of the Wounded Healers"—Peru

On the first day of our three-day pilgrimage to Machu Picchu in 2023, I stood at the base of the Salkantay Trek, embarking on a deeply transformative journey. The high-altitude air created a tapestry of sensations within me, weaving together irritability, anxiety, and profound apathy.

As I started climbing, I felt a strange transformation in my body. I felt compressed and expanded as if the landscape was molding my very being. This physical discomfort made me wonder why I was there and what this self-imposed challenge was for. The struggle with altitude was like a force that tested my mental and physical endurance, pushing me to my limits.

In this challenging journey, where comfort became a distant memory, I discovered an unexpected wellspring of strength. It came not from within but from being part of a collective experience, bearing witness to the vulnerabilities of my fellow travelers and listening deeply to the elemental voices of the mountains—the ancient rocks, the whispering winds, and the untamed spirits of the animals that called this majestic landscape home. It was a strength born from the unconventional proof of the symbiosis between humanity and the natural world.

Yet, amid the physical rigor and the mental strain of what appeared to be a never-ending journey, a dialogue unfolded with the Apus, the sacred mountain spirits of the Andes. Their presence, both commanding and ethereal, became a guiding force, a spectral conversation that transcended the familiar and ventured into the realm of the spirit. The mountains, ancient wisdom keepers, became mentors in perseverance, their rocky peaks whispering timeless tales of endurance to the weary travelers.

Standing amidst the mountains, I felt like I existed in both the physical and spiritual planes. It was a delicate balance that I had to navigate carefully. The rugged terrain of the mountains served as a symbolic bridge between these two realms. With each step I took, I felt like I was traversing the boundaries of ordinary existence and exploring new dimensions of reality.

By surrendering to the experience, I was able to attain a state of calmness. The altitude, once a challenge, became a means of embarking on a profound inner journey. Irritation transformed into resilience, anxiety into acceptance, and apathy into a quiet determination. It was as if the air held secrets, unlocking chambers of the soul dormant in the valleys below.

As I descended from the heights, the echoes of my transpersonal experience lingered. The Salkantay Trek was not just a physical challenge but a passage through the veils of existence, a mystical journey that left an indelible mark on my being. I emerged with not only blisters and sore muscles but also a transformed spirit, a feeling of being an essential part of nature's living mosaic. It was another testament to the profound alchemy that occurs when the human spirit recognizes itself in all creation.

As the day turned into night, I could not help but notice the distant and brilliant stars above. It made me realize that the vastness of the universe mirrored the dichotomy of my experience. I understood that growth often occurs when we push ourselves beyond our comfort zones.

Even though my body was protesting, and my mind was seeking solace, I could not help but feel that the cosmos was silently echoing the profound truth that transformation is a celestial dance that begins where familiarity ends.

This incredible journey through the Salkantay Trek went beyond just a physical expedition. It was a pilgrimage, a connection with the hidden forces that govern our existence's tangible and intangible aspects. Every step left a mark, every breath carried the whispers of ancient spirits, and every heartbeat synchronized with the earth's pulse.

VOICE OF THE PORTALS I: THE FIRST GATEWAY

"A Heroic Journey"—New Zealand

In December 2023, my husband and I embarked on a journey to explore the mystical landscapes of Aotearoa, New Zealand. Our adventure turned out to be an unexpected personal hero's journey, set against the backdrop of a land that seemed to be carved out of the pages of ancient myths and epic tales. It made me wonder if the fantastical narratives of fairy tales truly mirror the profound truths of life.

From the beginning, this enchanting land beckoned me to release my attachments to what I held dear, such as my habits and daily routines. In the embrace and honor of the local spirit, my physical and spiritual senses became vessels overflowing with the sheer abundance of beauty and the genuine kindness bestowed by the people.

As I journeyed further into this enchanting realm, it felt like the air was whispering ancient tales of heroism, and every step I took echoed the sounds of an epic quest. The landscapes, painted with colors borrowed from a mythical world, became the perfect backdrop for my personal odyssey. I was awestruck by the towering mountains, their grandeur evoking majestic ancient peaks, and the rolling hills reminding me of idyllic valleys gracefully formed by the sublime breath of creation.

The spirits of the land revealed themselves and their treasures in subtle whispers, inviting me to surrender to the enchantment of the moment. Amidst the valleys and meadows filled with vibrant aromatic flowers, I felt an intrinsic connection to the very essence of life, an acknowledgment that perhaps the threads of imagination, myth, and reality were intricately woven together.

The waters of this land reflected the dynamic nature of my journey, displaying an array of forms. The crystal glacier waters sparkled like the precious gems of fabled realms, while the sulfur hot springs emitted ancient energy akin to the fires of a legendary volcano. Along the shoreside, algae deposits released an intense aroma, a sensory journey mirroring life's complex layers and balance.

By a riverbank, rushing water spoke to me in ripples and murmurs. It whispered the wisdom that, like the untamed rivers, our divine innate nature is unchangeable and untouchable. At this moment, I realized the resonance with my exploration of self, an endeavor marked by the ebb and flow of personal transformation. Like the highest wizards of myth, humans possessed a unique magic—the power of choice and conscious intent.

The people of this land, embodying the spirit of fellowship, grew into characters in my unfolding narrative. Their warmth and genuine kindness transformed every encounter into a scene from an epic saga, reinforcing the belief that the elixir of heroes lies not in grand quests but in the shared humanity of everyday moments.

Culinary delights became a feast for the senses and the soul. The spirits of the land seemed to dance through the flavors, urging me to relinquish the rigid constraints of routine and embrace nourishment in all its forms. It was an invitation to savor each moment as a chapter in my heroine's journey, with the vibrant colors of nature infusing each bite with the magic of new possibilities.

Amidst the mythical echoes and the symphony of the natural world, I contemplated the seamless blend of fairy tales and reality. Perhaps the realms of imagination and the tangible world intertwine, suggesting that each step taken on this land was not merely physical but also a significant stride in the grand journey of my own life. It was a realization that the epic of personal transformation is not just about reaching a destination but embracing the journey itself. A journey filled with challenges, beauty, and the unfolding discovery of the hero within.

Reflections and Practices: Embracing Change

As we move from the colorful tapestry of my stories to a more contemplative space, I invite you to reflect on your life's transformative journeys. Each step, descent, celebration of life, and encounter with death shape us into who we are. These narratives, drawn from the depths of my soul and the corners of the earth, are mirrors that reflect our shared human experience of growth and change.

Through my journeys, I have learned that transformation is not a destination but an ongoing process, a continuous unfolding of the self. For example, my descent into the Initiation Well became a profound metaphor for my introspection.

Embracing the spiral descent into my being, navigating through darkness and light, and emerging reborn with a clearer understanding of myself. This story invites you to embrace your inner depths, trust the process of personal rebirth, and become more fully yourself.

The Salkantay Trek showed me that our scars are not signs of weakness but of healing and strength. This path, trodden by so many before us, symbolizes the pilgrimage of healing that we all must undertake. Here, vulnerability becomes our greatest strength, teaching us that healing is a journey, not a destination.

Journeying through New Zealand, I lived my hero's journey, confronting challenges, facing my dragons, and discovering deeper meanings in my quest. This adventure is a metaphor for our search for purpose and understanding, encouraging us to embrace our calls to adventure and return home transformed.

Navigating through life's myriad landscapes, both physical and emotional, offers us a profound opportunity for self-discovery and personal growth. By embracing change and journeying inward, we learn to navigate the complexities of our lives with a renewed sense of purpose and a deeper connection to the world around us.

Reflective Questions:

- Can you recall a moment when stepping out of your comfort zone led to a profound learning experience? What fears did you have to overcome, and how did this experience shape your understanding of yourself and the world around you?
- Can you think about a transformative journey (literal or metaphorical) you have taken recently? What new insights or understandings did you gain, and how have you integrated these into your daily life?
- In what ways has embracing vulnerability been a part of your transformative journeys? Describe a time when being vulnerable led to growth and change.

Inner Transformation: My Rituals of Change

On my personal development journey, I have discovered that rituals can have a transformative power that harnesses the forces of change, renewal, and personal evolution.

Based on the natural cycle of growth and rebirth, these practices serve as my compass through the landscapes of change, guiding me toward deeper self-awareness and resilience.

Here is an insight into the transformative rituals that have become pillars of strength in my quest for personal growth:

One Breath at a Time:

During my Salkantay Trek, an arduous journey marked by physical struggle and moments of doubt, I discovered the transformative power of taking life one breath at a time. This experience taught me a valuable lesson that extends beyond the mountains.

Whether facing a steep climb, waiting in line, or being entangled in an argument, each breath offers a chance to pause, reconnect with the present moment, and navigate life's challenges gracefully.

I integrate this practice into my daily routine as much as possible, treating each breath as a touchstone, a reminder of the constant flow of life and the cycles that shape our existence.

By focusing on my breath, I find calm in chaos and clarity in uncertainty, embodying the resilience and adaptability that the trek instilled in me. This mindful approach to breathwork, supported by its well-documented benefits for stress reduction and mental clarity, serves as a daily ritual of inner transformation, guiding me through life's terrain with the same courage and steadiness that carried me through the Salkantay Trek.

Creating Personal Rituals of Transformation:

I have found immense value in crafting personal rituals to mark key transitions in my life. These rituals are simple yet profound ways of acknowledging change, celebrating growth, and setting intentions for the future. They serve as tangible milestones on my path of personal evolution, helping me to honor the moments of letting go, welcoming new beginnings, and reflecting on my journey. Here is how I approach this practice:

1. **Identifying Transitions:** First, I recognize the moments or phases in my life that represent a transition. These could be anything from changing jobs, moving homes, ending or beginning a relationship, or personal achievements and milestones. Each moment offers an opportunity for reflection, new insights, gratitude, and celebration.
2. **Crafting the Ritual:** With the transition identified, I craft a simple ritual that feels meaningful to me. This could involve lighting a candle to symbolize the light of awareness and hope, writing a letter to my future self, or creating a small altar with objects that represent what I am letting go of and what I am moving toward.
3. **Setting Intentions:** During the ritual, I set clear intentions for the next phase of my journey. This might involve verbal affirmations, meditation, or writing my hopes and goals down in a journal. The key is to focus my thoughts and energy on the positive outcomes I wish to manifest.

4. **Celebrating the Moment:** Finally, I celebrate the transition by acknowledging the growth and learning that brought me to this point. This celebration can be as simple as sharing a meal with loved ones, taking a solitary walk in nature, or any activity that brings joy and closure to the old chapter while welcoming the new.

Creating personal rituals for life's transitions is more than a symbolic act; it is a practice grounded in our psychological and emotional needs. These rituals can anchor us, providing clarity, comfort, and a renewed sense of purpose during times of change.

My rituals of transformation have become a vital part of my journey. They offer a flexible and meaningful way to honor the rites of passage that define my life. This practice can be adapted to fit any circumstance or phase of life, reminding us of our resilience, capacity for growth, and the ever-present opportunity for renewal.

Crafting My Epic:

Using the hero's journey as a framework, I have chronicled my life's pivotal moments, recognizing them as chapters in my epic. This method illuminates my path through trials, transformations, and triumphs, mapping a story of resilience and growth.

In this crafted narrative, every challenge becomes a call to adventure, every setback an opportunity, and every achievement a return home with newfound wisdom. This approach transforms my experiences into a mythic journey, granting me perspective and strength.

By reflecting on my journey this way, I see myself not just as a participant in life but as an active creator of my story, drawing on the universal hero's journey to navigate the world's complexities with courage and insight.

Research suggests that framing life as a heroic journey can significantly impact our psychological well-being, providing a structure for personal growth and resilience.

Historically, this mirrors the archetypal narratives in many cultures, where the hero's journey is a metaphor for the individual's path of self-discovery and transformation.

By incorporating these practices into my life, I have connected with ancient traditions and modern psychological insights and discovered a profound sense of belonging and purpose. These rituals are more than just personal habits; they are evidence of our human capacity for resilience and transformation.

As we navigate life's journey, personalized rituals illuminate our path, offering clarity and purpose amid the complexities of modern existence. By consciously marking each transition, we fully engage with the rich tapestry of human experience, allowing us to step into our true selves with courage and grace.

Sharing these practices, I hope to inspire you to explore and establish your personal or family rituals, enhancing your narrative of growth and transformation.

As this chapter on "Journeys of Transformation" draws to a close, let us embrace the powerful notion that our life's journey is punctuated with sacred rites of passage, compelling us to acknowledge, be grateful, and celebrate the evolution of our heroic journey.

As we wrap up our reflections and practices on journeys of transformation, a path rich with personal growth and self-discovery, we stand on the brink of venturing further into the mystic, toward encounters with the unseen.

The transformations we have navigated were not just passages through physical landscapes but also gateways into the depths of our being, where the boundaries of our understanding begin to blur.

Now, armed with the insights and strengths gleaned from these transformative experiences, we are prepared to explore the realms that lie beyond the tangible.

The unseen awaits with lessons hidden in the shadows and whispers from beyond, inviting us to expand our consciousness and embrace the mysteries that challenge our perceptions of reality. With hearts open to the profound and eyes keen for the invisible, we step forward, ready to encounter the wonders and wisdom residing in the spaces between.

CHAPTER III

ENCOUNTERS WITH THE UNSEEN

"The best and most beautiful things in the world cannot be seen or even touched; they must be felt with the heart."
—*Helen Keller.*

Let us go on a journey beyond the tangible into the realms where the known meets the unknown. A place where the ancient whispers echo in the silence of the night and where the mysteries of the cosmos unfold before our very eyes. This chapter invites us to explore those rare moments and sacred sites that challenge our understanding of reality and compel us to question what lies beyond the reach of our physical senses.

Have you ever felt the presence of something greater than yourself, a force unseen yet palpably alive in the air around you? Perhaps it was in a moment of solitude amidst the grandeur of nature, under the vast, starry sky, or within the silent walls of a place steeped in ancient history.

These experiences, often fleeting and unbidden, connect us to the infinite tapestry of existence that extends beyond our immediate perception.

As we journey through the ancient, stirring landscapes of Uluru and Kata Tjuta in Australia, we touch the sacred ground where the Dreamtime stories of creation are etched into the earth. We are invited to listen deeply to the song lines that crisscross the land.

In the shadowy recesses of the Ana Kai Tangata Cave in Rapa Nui, we peer into the depths where ancient civilizations sought to bridge the world of the living and the spirits. What messages do these ancestral symbols have for us today?

Over five thousand miles away, our journey takes us to the geometric alignments of Washington, DC, where the layout of a modern city hints at a deeper, star-aligned mystery. What unseen forces guided the hands that drew these lines, connecting the earth with the celestial?

In Evora, Portugal, as we merge with the unseen energies, we are reminded of the intricate dance of the universe, a reminder that everything is interconnected, every star, every stone, and every soul a note in a grander melody.

Each narrative in this chapter is not just a recounting of travels to places where the veil thins but an invitation to reflect on your encounters with the unseen. Have you sensed the delicate fabric of reality warp, even for a moment, to reveal a glimpse of something extraordinary? These encounters beckon us to open our minds and hearts to the possibility that there is much more to this existence than meets the eye.

"Encounters with the Unseen" explores the sacred thresholds where the material and the mystical meet, urging us to question, seek, and wonder. It is a journey into the heart of the mysteries surrounding us, a gentle nudge to acknowledge the unseen forces shaping our lives and the universe.

As we venture forth, let us do so with a sense of wonder, curiosity, and a beginner's mind, ready to be transformed by the mysteries that await.

"Playing in the Cosmic Symphony"—Portugal

During my pilgrimage in 2022, I ventured to the ancient grounds of Almedres Crómlech in Portugal, embarking on a journey beyond the veil of the visible. As I crossed this metaphorical bridge, shrouded in mist, the anticipation of what lay beyond filled me with a deep sense of surrender and curiosity.

Almedres Crómlech, a place of immense power and mystery, welcomed me into its embrace. The ancient stones, sculpted by time, stood as silent guardians of an ethereal energy that seemed almost palpable. With its unique aura, each stone seemed to vibrate in harmony with the natural world, revealing an unseen dance of light and shadow.

Hesitantly, I reached out to touch one of the megaliths, and a silent symphony began to play upon contact. The stones, each singing a different note, created a melody that resonated through the air and within my soul. With every touch, I was transported beyond time into a realm where the past, present, and future merged. Here, amidst the standing stones, time loses its grip, and I immersed myself in the eternal now.

I realized that these stones are not merely relics of the past and silent witnesses. They are active participants; each of their unique songs echoed through the air, resonating with every cell in my body. The energy they exude is a language, a vibration that transcends spoken words. It communicates a profound connection to the Earth, to the cosmos, and to the very essence of existence.

I became attuned to their silent conversations as I danced among the stones. Each one carried a story etched in its ancient surface, a tale of times long past and mysteries that transcend human understanding. The air was charged with an otherworldly ambiance, and I felt as though I was partaking in dialogue with forces beyond comprehension.

Here, I felt an unusual energy in the air and became aware of subtle vibrations around me. It was not just the stones resonating; the entire landscape seemed to be humming with a frequency beyond ordinary perception. It was like a natural symphony and cosmic harmony that transcended what we could see. I found myself pondering, "Can I hear and feel my frequency? Can I allow my unique vibration to play along?"

The mist surrounding Almedres Crómlech acted as a veil between worlds, adding an ethereal touch to the enchanting scene. It obscured the boundaries between the seen and the unseen, inviting me to venture further into the unknown. With each step, the mist enveloped me, and the boundary between self and surroundings became fluid, as if I were merging with this mystical place's essence.

Emerging from the mist, I carried with me the melody of the stones, a song of unity and eternal presence. Almedres Crómlech had revealed its secrets not through words but through the profound language of vibration, inviting me to listen with more than my ears and to feel with more than my heart. This mystical encounter transformed me, reminding me that we are all part of a greater, cosmic symphony, playing our unique notes in the dance of existence.

"Stillness"—Rapa Nui

In October 2023, I went on my second pilgrimage to Easter Island, this time with my sisterhood. The first time I visited the Island was back in 2002 with my husband. During this recent visit, we were particularly drawn to the enigmatic Ana Kai Tangata Cave. Unlike my first visit, I approached the cave with a blend of eagerness and learned confidence. This time,

VOICE OF THE PORTALS I: THE FIRST GATEWAY

I came equipped with tools and teachings acquired over the years, ready to engage with the cave's dissonant energies anew.

The cave's inner walls revealed ancient art, not just the mere creations of human hands, but rather etchings from the very soul of the earth. Dragons, snakes, and serpent-like people adorned the stone, custodians of treasured memories—both dreadful and joyous. As timeless symbols, the petroglyphs captured the depth of transcendent moments, evading the limitations of spoken words. Everything here had a language beyond time, inviting me to feel and decipher the codes within my existence. In the presence of these symbols, I found myself not merely an observer but a participant in a history narrative.

Amidst these symbols, a realization unfurled, and I questioned the validity of my spoon-fed beliefs. Whose stories am I accepting to be my truth? Like the cave, my mind prompted me to explore its dark crevasses. Each perception, after all, is born from inner experiences. To gain a new perspective, I moved fluidly within and around the cave, shedding the constraints of my own stories, beliefs, and personal agendas.

A mysterious voice interrupted my wandering, "Just sit," it echoed, catching me off guard. "Nothing to do but to sit, just be." The cave's riddling guidance led me to a profound understanding: inner stillness is the altar of spirit. To sit within my frequency was the essence of true numinosity. The cave beckoned me to be still and recognize that genuine change emanates from the observer, not the observed.

Amid the flickering shadows, a shift occurred within me. The cave's resistance was not a rejection but a call to inner exploration. The symbols on the walls pulsed with life, telling stories of creation, destruction, and the eternal nature of existence. Like ancient scribes, the petroglyphs chronicled the evolution of consciousness, leaving an indelible mark on the cavern's soul. And like the cave, we possess the potential to embrace the spectrum of creation without becoming entwined in its carvings.

As I immersed myself in this timeless narrative, a mysterious voice resonated again through the cavern. "In stillness, you find the keys to the universe," it whispered. The guidance echoed through the chambers, prompting me to continue the contemplation. With each passing moment of silence, the cave's energy merged with mine, revealing another profound truth—I was not here to conquer but to commune, to listen to the earth's heartbeat echoing through the stones.

Weaving my way in and out of the cave, the dissonance transformed into understanding. While the petroglyphs whispered timeless tales, I grasped the essence of contrast and self-discernment. By choosing stillness and neutrality, I transcended the limitations of my perceived reality. The cave, a silent teacher, reminded me that within the vastness of existence, our true power lies not in insisting on changing the external but in the persistent commitment to evolve and transform ourselves by choosing the lens through which we perceive.

As I delved into the heart of Rapa Nui, Ana Kai Tangata Cave became a sacred vessel, carrying the echoes of ancient wisdom. Once a barrier, the dissonance became a threshold to a realm beyond my conventional understanding. Once perceived as unwelcoming, the cave's energy now revealed itself as a mirror reflecting the depths of my being.

In this dance of shadows and light, fears and revelations, the mystical journey within the cave became a profound exploration of my human experience, acknowledging and embracing the potential for both dark and light within. The ancient art on the cave's walls guided me to recognize the symbols within and taught me that true magic lies in understanding and embracing the ever-changing, contrasting aspects of existence. The realization that the cave was not just a physical space but a portal to self-discovery resonated deeply, pushing the story further into the realms of introspection.

Emerging from the cave, I carried the reverberance of its sacred teachings. The dissonance that initially greeted me transformed into a symphony of interconnected energies. The cave, once perceived as a dark, isolated space, now a harmonious melody, echoed in my every step, a reminder that transformation begins from within.

The petroglyphs, radiant with ancient wisdom, now etched in my consciousness, continued to whisper their infinite treasured stories.

On my return pilgrimage with my sisterhood, Ana Kai Tangata Cave unveiled itself as a profound teacher. It reminded me that the journey of understanding and integration is an inward voyage, where the magic of existence is revealed through the dance of contrasting energies and the stillness of our inner being.

"Awaken Dreamwalkers"—*Australia*

In late November 2023, I embarked on a solo journey to the heart of Australia, drawn to the magnetic allure of Uluru. My adventure began with a whirlwind of uncertainty, narrowly making my connecting flight, which set the tone for an experience guided by the flow of the universe rather than any meticulously laid plans.

Upon arrival, nature's elements welcomed me with a majestic display of their might. The desert sun, a fiery ball in the expansive sky, cast its warm glow upon the ancient red earth. A swirl of air whispered tales of ages past, carrying the scent of wet red dirt that vibrated with the memories of countless pilgrimages along the dreaming tracks of our ancestors.

Rain unexpectedly fell from gray clouds, inviting me to join nature's symphony.

As I walked, the bird's wings created a rhythmic vibration, harmonizing with the steps of natives and visitors alike. It was as if the land, the people, and all creatures were orchestrating a one-field symphony, beckoning me to listen with more than just my ears. This was a waking dream where the echoes of ancient tales echoed in the ears of the new wisdom keepers of the Earth.

Amidst this sensory overload, whispers of guidance gently reached my awareness: "Listen carefully; allow the wisdom to permeate from your ears into your mind and settle in your heart." It was an invitation to transcend the ordinary and consider Uluru as a primordial portal to interdimensional gateways.

"Time to wake up, dreamwalker," the whispers continued, resonating with a magnetic and polarizing feeling. Despite the struggle with the desert heat and the persistent jet lag, I sensed a watchful presence, as if an elder guide was silently overseeing my well-being. "Slow down; you have eternity," echoed a voice, and at that moment, the boundaries between wakefulness and dream began to blur.

As I continued, my physical body entered a dreamlike state. An energy circuit connected the stars above, through Uluru, diving deep into the earth, flowing up through the soles of my feet, cascading out from my crown, and returning to the stars. The essence of existence seemed to pulse through me and this sacred site, weaving together the threads of the universe into a tapestry of interconnected energies.

Nearby, Kata Tjuta, with its domed formations, appeared like silhouettes gazing at the stars. Here, I felt embraced by a universal harmonious field, a delicate balance between worlds that transcended the limitations of my mind. It was as if the rocks themselves held the secrets, whispering tales of cosmic serpents spiraling around, protecting a precious mother dragon's egg.

As I was leaving, I felt as though some unseen force was guiding me. I noticed signs and symbols related to serpent energy all around me, such as the bus driver telling his story about surviving a snake bite and the Aboriginal elder pointing out serpent-like dunes. The pulsating hypnotic sound of a didgeridoo playing in the distance made me realize the deep connection between the sacred land and my existence.

Finally, I was silently reminded to respect the delicate balance of nature with the words, "Leave no-thing; take no-thing."

Departing from Uluru and Kata Tjuta, I carried with me the stories and wisdom of this ancient land and a deep sense of connection to the larger cosmos. This journey, undertaken in solitude, revealed that here, at the very heart of Australia, the veil between the waking world and the realm of dreams is thin, and we are all woven into the cosmic field that binds us to the earth and each other.

"Interstellar Capitol"—Washington D.C.

In December 2023, I found myself in Washington, D.C., visiting our daughter, who was immersed in the seasonal excitement of a show she was part of.

The festive energy of the holidays provided a stark contrast to the mystical journey I was about to embark upon in the heart of our nation's capital. As a seeker of the unseen, drawn to the city not just for familial ties but for its rich tapestry of history and hidden mysteries, I felt the pulse of ancient energies and secrets whispering through the cool breeze.

My exploration began at the base of the Washington Monument. This towering obelisk, a familiar landmark against the crisp winter sky, acted as a conduit between earthly realms and celestial spaces.

Touching its cold, smooth surface, I was transported to the sands of ancient Egypt and the cryptic knowledge of the Templars. This structure, I realized, was more than a mere memorial; it was a crucial piece in the cosmic puzzle that the city's layout presented, a key to the energetic ley lines that converged beneath my feet.

Venturing onward, the Capitol Building awaited with its grandeur and underlying enigmas. The architectural marvel spoke in a hidden language of symbols, a dialogue of sacred geometry that whispered of the city's Masonic influences. It was as if each column and archway carried the weight of untold stories, aligning not just with the founding fathers' vision but with the very stars above.

The setting sun led me to the Lincoln Memorial, where time seemed to stand still, bridging the gap between the tangible and the mystical. The precise alignment of this monument with others in the city did not seem coincidental but rather part of a deliberate design, a star map crafted in marble and pathways, channeling the potent energies of the earth.

As darkness began to envelop the city, the Jefferson Memorial called to me, its silhouette reflecting on the tranquil waters before it. Here, at the water's edge, the boundary between worlds felt permeable, and I glimpsed into the realm of parallel existences, a place where other dimensions brushed up against our own.

At nightfall, signaling the end of my city pilgrimage, I emerged from Washington, D.C.'s hidden layers with a newfound connection to its esoteric blueprint. The city's landmarks, symbols of political might and national pride, had revealed their deeper purpose to me. They served as markers on a journey beyond the physical, aligning with celestial patterns, resonating with the Earth's energies, and beckoning to the curious soul willing to look beyond the veil.

This visit, coinciding with the festive reunion with our daughter, intertwined the personal with the mystical, leaving me with a profound appreciation for Washington, D.C.'s role as a portal between the seen and unseen, a capital not just of a country but perhaps of interstellar gateways.

Reflections and Practices: Beyond the Veil

As we delve deeper into the essence of "Encounters with the Unseen," we uncover not just stories of ancient wonders and mystical sites but also a pathway to integrating these encounters into our daily lives. Each narrative serves as a beacon, illuminating the sacredness embedded in our existence and challenging us to perceive the beauty and mystery beyond the edge of our visible reality.

In Evora, the celestial harmonies that resonate through ancient megalithic sites teach us that every stone, every being, is a note in the grand cosmic symphony. This tale encourages us to listen to the universe's music, to find harmony within ourselves and our place within the vastness of existence.

Within the silent embrace of the Ana Kai Tangata Cave, we are reminded of the profound stillness within and around us—a stillness that allows us to hear the subtle voices of the unseen world. This narrative encourages us to seek moments of silence in our lives, to find spaces where we can disconnect from everyday noise and listen to past and present whispers.

In the heart of Australia, the ancient spirits of the land beckon to us to walk in dreams, introducing us to the sacred practice of Dreamtime. It is more than a story; it is an invitation to connect with the wisdom of the Earth and our ancestors. This ancient tradition teaches us the power of listening deeply to the stories that the land itself wants to tell us, urging us to find ways to incorporate this listening into our everyday lives.

The hidden astrological and esoteric symbols within the layout of Washington, D.C., revealed to me a city designed to mirror the sky. This story opens our eyes to the ancient knowledge and cosmic connections that influence the modern world, inviting us to consider how these alignments affect our lives and perceptions.

These stories and the lessons they carry teach us that the unseen is not to be feared but embraced with curiosity as a source of wisdom, strength, and inspiration. They invite us to reflect on our moments of connection with the invisible forces that shape our lives.

Whether through feelings, insights, or dreams, our encounters with the unseen enrich our existence, guiding, inspiring, and challenging us in equal measure.

Reflective Questions:

- Have you ever felt the presence of something beyond the physical world? Describe the experience and how it impacted you.

- What unseen energies are you most curious about, and how might you open yourself to learning more about them?

Connecting to the Unseen: My Pathway to Mystery

In exploring the unseen, I have cultivated practices that allow me to touch the intangible and connect with the mysterious energies that dance beyond our ordinary perception.

Approaching these practices with curiosity and a beginner's mind, I embrace the wonder of acknowledging how much lies beyond my understanding. Here is a look into the practices that have become gateways for me to the unseen realms:

Inner Journeys:

Daily, I carve out moments to sit quietly in a space dedicated to reflection and connection. Here, I close my eyes and transport myself to the sacred landscapes, sites, or memories that hold a special place in my heart. I feel their energy, imagine the sounds and scents, and let this visualization bridge the gap between me and the unseen.

This practice reminds me that, though physically apart, we are always energetically connected to others and these powerful places.

Visualization practices have a rich history in various spiritual traditions and are supported by contemporary psychology research. Studies show that visualization can significantly affect the brain's plasticity, leading to changes in behavior, thoughts, and emotions.

Visualizing, especially within spaces designated for reflection and connection, can enhance one's sense of presence and mindfulness, supporting a well-documented pathway to stress reduction and improved well-being.

Dreamscape Chronicles:

Besides my bed, a journal awaits the whispers of my soul's desires. Each morning, I record my dreamtime adventures. Dreams, for me, are portals to the unseen realms, offering unlimited potential for adventures, insights, healing, and wisdom.

By paying attention to these nightly narratives, I deepen my connection to the unseen world, learning to navigate its symbols and signs with curiosity and respect.

The practice of honoring dreams dates back to ancient cultures and has been a pivotal part of understanding the human psyche in modern psychology. Contemporary research validates the value of dream journaling in enhancing creativity, problem-solving skills, and emotional processing.

By paying attention to the symbolic language of our dreams, we can gain insights into our unconscious mind, potentially leading to greater self-awareness and personal development in our waking life.

My Inner Sanctum: Personal Check-Ins:

I regularly allocate time to retreat into solitude, stepping away from the constant buzz of the digital world to reconnect with myself and the unseen.

These personal half-day or full-day retreats are sacred times of meditation, contemplation, and silence, where I can listen more deeply to the subtle energies inside and surrounding me. In these undistracted moments, I often find profound insights and strengthen my bond with the unseen.

The tradition of retreats is deeply rooted in many spiritual and religious practices, offering a time for introspection, meditation, and reconnection with the unseen aspects of our existence. Scientific studies support the benefits of such practices, showing that periods of silence and meditation can significantly reduce stress, improve cognitive functions, and enhance one's overall sense of well-being.

The modern digital detox movement, advocating for intentional breaks from technology, aligns with this ancient wisdom. It highlights the importance of disconnecting from external distractions to reconnect with one's inner world and the subtle energies of the Earth and Universe.

Emerging from our encounters with the unseen, where the veil between the worlds thinned, and the whispers of the ancients guided us, we carry forward a newfound reverence for the mysteries that dance in the shadowed corners of our existence. And, as we transition from the ethereal realms of the unseen to the vibrant tapestry of life that surrounds us, let us open our hearts to the laughter and lessons that await.

CHAPTER IV

GUARDIANS OF WISDOM AND LAUGHTER

"Laughter is the sun that drives winter from the human face."
—Victor Hugo.

Let us embark on a journey highlighting the vibrant interplay between joy and profundity. Wisdom is not imparted in solemn tones but through the universal language of laughter and light-heartedness.

This chapter invites you to discover stories where the sacred is celebrated in quiet reverence and moments of joy, playfulness, and spontaneous connection, highlighting our shared human experience.

Throughout my travels and quest for understanding, wisdom has often appeared in unexpected forms and teachers. Whether it was through a naughty encounter with cucarachas on the mystical island of Rapa Nui, the wild whispering guidance of Aotearoa's animal kingdom, or the silent wisdom of its enchanting plant life, I have learned that wisdom often wears the disguise of joy and laughter.

These experiences have shown me that our connections with nature and the myriad creatures with whom we share this planet can be profound sources of insight and enlightenment.

Each story within this chapter is a testament to the idea that laughter and joy are not mere distractions on the path to understanding but are integral companions that guide us toward deeper truths. The guardians of wisdom, it turns out, are often those we least expect.

By sharing these light-hearted yet profound encounters, I hope to remind us that the journey toward wisdom can be filled with laughter, joy, and the celebration of life in all its forms.

The guardians of wisdom and laughter await us in every corner of our lives, ready to teach us, to connect with us, and to remind us of the beauty of our shared humanity. Let us embrace these moments, for in them lies the true essence of understanding and connection.

"Mystical Realms"—New Zealand

During our romp through New Zealand, my husband and I found ourselves entranced by the whimsical realms of Aotearoa, the native name of New Zealand. This land, rich with the whispers of ages past, unfolded its tales before us, not like a solemn history book but more like a pop-up book of fantastical stories. Guided by the earth's silent songs, we ventured into the magical flora. Each native tree, lupin, and flower seemed to leap out of a fairy tale, inviting us to a dance where the language went beyond mere words.

As we meandered through the forest, the ground seemed to buzz with a life of its own. The mycelium network below orchestrated a symphony of magical fungi and vibrant moss, choreographing a dance with the roots of towering sequoias. These ancient trees, standing tall like the wizened elders of the forest, seemed to wink at us, sharing their millennia-old jokes.

At Monro Creek Beach Forest, it felt as if we had stepped into a secret garden party hosted by the plant kingdom's most ethereal beings.

Elementals and spirits seemed to flit about, some shyly peeking from behind leaves, others boldly introducing themselves as the land's ancient custodians. "Through my silence, come hear my story," whispered a voice, not solemn but invitingly, like an old friend sharing a secret over a cup of tea. In this moment, a realization dawned on me: we are all part of this grand, interconnected web woven together with threads of stories and laughter.

Amidst these ancient trees, I discovered nature's sense of humor. Staring at a particularly gnarled tree, an unexpected laugh bubbled up within me. The plant kingdom, with its silent wisdom, taught me the value of laughter and joy—a universal language that connects us deeply to the Earth and each other.

The trails and tunnels of Woods Creek were alive with the playful spirits of nature, guiding me not just through the physical landscape but through a journey of discovery and connection. Surrounded by trees, I could not help but feel like the central character in a whimsical play, the forest stage set for my transformation from mere observer to active participant in nature's grand narrative.

Leaving this enchanted realm, my thoughts wandered to the adventures that lay ahead and the mysteries of consciousness yet to be explored. Watching the diverse crowd of visitors, I was struck by a profound sense of unity—a realization that nature, with its universal language of beauty and wonder, can bring us all together in a shared dance of awe, joy, and discovery.

In Aotearoa's embrace, every plant, from the majestic to the smallest, became a beacon of light-hearted wisdom, whispering secrets not with the seriousness of sages but with the sparkle of storytellers eager to share. The entire landscape was a stage for nature's play, where every leaf, stone, and ray of sunlight held a part in the cosmic comedy of life.

And so, we left, our hearts lighter for the laughter shared with the ancient guardians of Aotearoa. We were reminded that wisdom often comes wrapped in joy and that laughter is, indeed, the music of the soul.

"Settle in the Stones"—New Zealand

During our delightful adventure through New Zealand in December 2023, we stumbled upon nature's art gallery at the Omarama Clay Cliffs. These cliffs, painting the sky with their ochre strokes, seemed to chuckle in the sunlight as if amused by their own grandeur. In a moment of playful creativity, it was as if the Earth herself had sculpted these formations just to see our astonished faces.

Our trek on the clay ground was accompanied by the wind's peculiar howls through the peaks, a natural symphony with its own rhythm and beat. The rocks along our path were not just silent guardians of ancient tales but appeared to us as mischievous storytellers, each eager to share its piece of Earth's ancient gossip.

By the time we reached Lake Wakatipu, the land had thoroughly charmed us. The gold mines, now silent, seemed to whisper cheeky secrets of their glittering past, urging us to lean closer. Each jade stone under our touch felt like a green-thumbed wizard, eager to impart lessons of resilience with a wink.

The real surprise awaited us at Kura Tāwhiti, Castle Hill, where the so-called silent stones turned out to be the life of nature's party. The smaller rocks, perhaps tired of being overshadowed by their towering companions, revealed their quirky characters, proving that greatness truly comes in all sizes.

Climbing a hill to meet the goddess Marotini, we half-expected a solemn monument. Instead, we found a celestial rockstar, her form against the stars, striking a pose that seemed to say, "The universe's creation? Oh, just another day's work for me." Under her watchful gaze, we picnicked, and the stones around us whispered not with the solemnity of old sages but with the giggles of ancient children reminding us, "Life's too vast to take too seriously."

Preparing to leave, we realized the giant stones had played the greatest trick of all; their majestic presence was a dazzling misdirection from the hidden treasures beneath our feet.

A playful realization struck me in the heart of Aotearoa amidst its vast landscapes: the essence of the "eternal child" lives vividly in the natural world. This concept, often found in myths, manifested through the land's playfulness, urging us to embrace life with wonder and joy.

The laughter of streams and the playful dance of the breeze reminded us that amidst life's solemn lessons, there is always space for light-heartedness and the pure delight of being. This revelation, gifted by New Zealand, transformed our journey into a celebration of life's unending youthfulness and the joy of discovery, embodying the eternal child's spirit in every moment.

"Whispers of the Wild"—New Zealand

Reflecting on my experiences with the animal kingdom in New Zealand, December 2023, I feel honored.

Ever since I was a child, I have been passionate about animals and have volunteered as a rescuer. Writing about these amazing creatures feels like a sacred duty to me.

Aotearoa is a land full of Māori legends and natural beauty. Being there allowed me to connect with the wisdom of the animal kingdom. The pastures were a vibrant tapestry of life, where sheep grazed peacefully under the watchful eyes of shepherd dogs. Cows and deer also coexisted with them in a seamless dance of life.

As I stood there, I could not help but marvel at the beauty of the animals and how they were interconnected with humans through wool and flesh. Suddenly, an inner calling emerged within me. I yearned to connect with the land and taste the animals that roamed the green pastures.

This was a profound step for me, as it contrasted greatly with my ingrained culinary habits. The call to commune with the essence of the land became a symbolic stepping stone, urging me to reevaluate my relationship with sustenance.

While driving, searching for a tourist spot, I found myself lost and going in circles. Suddenly, I came across a lone horse patiently waiting for me. It felt like the horse invited me to stop, get closer, and enjoy being human. The horse's gaze seemed to say: "Life is beautiful; slow down and savor it." It made me realize that I had become so absorbed in my pursuit of wisdom that I had forgotten to enjoy the simple things in life. Perhaps the journey to enlightenment is about lighting up and allowing myself to enjoy each moment.

As I walked down the path, I encountered three little piggies exploring their surroundings with childlike curiosity. Their carefree attitude reminded me to cherish the simple pleasures in life.

While cruising through a beautiful landscape, I stumbled upon a group of curious and friendly cows. They rushed toward me with unbridled joy, and their energy and happiness were so infectious that they awakened a vitality within me. It was a moment of pure bliss and connection, reminding me that joy is a fundamental aspect of the human experience that the complexities of life can sometimes overshadow.

As I followed the ethereal traces of the Hasst's Eagle, my journey continued with a special encounter with a couple of kiwis. Each kiwi represents a primordial piece of the mystical puzzle, Aotearoa.

Playful keas, ducks, wekas, doves, robins, and bats added their unique melodies to the symphony of nature. Graceful swans glided with elegance while seagulls soared with unapologetic freedom, embodying the spirit of living authentically without any compromise. Amidst this avian serenade, I had a warm encounter with a stray feline. Despite being weathered and worn, the cat offered me its affection unconditionally. This unexpected warmth echoed the notion that connection transcends appearances. It served as a reminder of the unconditional love that threads through the innate core of all beings.

As I watched bumblebees go about their business with incredible resilience and perseverance, I realized just how crucial they are to the delicate web of life. Their constant, almost invisible movement from one flower to another highlighted the interdependence of all living beings. Even the bothersome sand flies, though often seen as a nuisance, played an important part in maintaining the balance of the ecosystem.

The whispers of the animal kingdom spoke to me, reminding me that we are all connected. They encouraged me to enjoy life without apologizing or compromising too much.

Every being has a unique role to play in the grand tapestry of existence, which can only be achieved through collaboration and harmony. Recognizing this interconnectedness has helped me find a deep sense of belonging.

In the magical realms of Aotearoa, the animal kingdom revealed secrets of Waitaha's legends and passed along keys to unlock a harmonious existence. I learned that the most spiritual thing I could do was to fully enjoy being human. As I left the pastures behind, the lessons lingered, a melody of connection, joy, endurance, and authenticity echoing in the winds. These lessons will guide me, and I am honored to carry the wisdom of the animal kingdom into my own life.

"Namaskar Cucaracha"—Rapa Nui

During my pilgrimage in October 2023, amidst the sacred backdrop of Rapa Nui, I encountered an unexpected and transformative experience.

Surrounded by the stoic Moai statues, my journey took an amusing turn as I found myself amidst cucarachas, those creatures I had always been programmed to fear.

While exploring the ancient landscape, I could not help but notice the presence of cucarachas (cockroaches), which triggered a cascade of childhood memories loaded with learned aversions.

Programming has always obscured my perception of these creatures like an invisible veil. However, determined to unravel this deeply ingrained fear, I decided to confront it amidst the enigmatic stones and the laughter shared with my companions.

On a quiet spot among the Moais, I settled into contemplation, the rhythmic sounds of the ocean waves serving as a soothing backdrop. In this tranquil moment, I spot a cucaracha, its swift movements invoking a reflexive shiver. Instead of succumbing to the programmed response, I decided to laugh—a burst of spontaneous, genuine laughter that echoed through the ancient rocks.

Laughter became my unexpected support mechanism, a liberating force that dismantled the walls of fear built in childhood. I observed the cucaracha with newfound curiosity, its small form taking on a whimsical charm as I embodied this tiny and intricate expression of life itself.

The Moais, seemingly guardians of the island's wisdom, stood tall as witnesses to this transformation, their stoic expressions softening in the glow of realization.

With each passing day, my laughter became a constant companion, accentuating the playful dance of the cucarachas. I found myself laughing not at them but with them, acknowledging their role in the intricate dance of existence. It became a shared laughter, a celebration of the interconnectedness between all living beings.

Once a rigid framework, childhood programming began to dissolve in the laughter-infused air. The Moais, as silent companions, seemed to nod approvingly at this newfound freedom. Laughter became the alchemy that transformed fear into understanding, rigidity into fluidity, and aversion into acceptance.

The laughter, now a part of the island's energy, weaves into the fabric of the universe. The cucarachas, once perceived as harbingers of discomfort, became symbols of resilience and adaptability, their movements a rhythmic dance beneath the starry night sky.

As the days unfolded, an unforeseen challenge arose, testing the boundaries of my newfound acceptance. Faced

VOICE OF THE PORTALS I: THE FIRST GATEWAY

with the growing presence of cucarachas in my living space, a moment of reflex took hold, and I found myself wielding a broom, not in laughter, but in a battle against the very creatures I had come to view through a lens of amusement.

This act, a departure from my committed path of "Do no-harm," stirred a deep internal conflict. It was a stark reminder of my own complexity and the layers of conditioning still to be unraveled.

This moment, as conflicting as it was, became yet another teacher on my journey. It forced me to confront the shadows within to acknowledge that the path to self-acceptance is filled with contradictions. Accepting all aspects of myself meant recognizing the existence of both light and darkness and understanding that growth is a non-linear process.

Reflecting upon this experience under the stoic gaze of the Moais, I realized that true transformation involves embracing the full spectrum of our humanity—our kindness and impulses, our laughter, and our fears.

This humbling lesson in Rapa Nui taught me that the journey toward wholeness is not about achieving perfection but about striving for authenticity, acknowledging our failings, learning from them, and eventually laughing with them.

As I bid farewell to the mystical landscapes of Rapa Nui, the laughter and the moments of conflict intertwined, leaving me with a profound understanding of our intricate human experience.

The cucarachas, once simple symbols of fear transformed into laughter, now represented a deeper truth about the human condition—the ongoing dance between our ideals and our actions, between acceptance and resistance.

Reflections and Practices: The Lighter Side of Spirit

As we journey through the narratives, we find ourselves at the crossroads of wisdom and laughter, where the stories of our interactions with the natural world remind us of the profound lessons learned in joy and delight. Reflecting on these tales, I invite you to ponder your own experiences.

Have you ever been taught an unexpected lesson by the laughter shared with a friend, the whimsy of an animal companion, or the serene beauty of a plant thriving against all odds? These guardians of wisdom and laughter in our lives urge us to view our existence through a lens of joy, wonder, and a deeper appreciation.

My journey has been sprinkled with these light-hearted mentors, who have taught me to cherish the present moment, find joy in the simplest of interactions, and pay attention to the wisdom of our non-human companions. From the humility learned from cheeky cucarachas to the sense of kinship felt with the wild animals of New Zealand, each encounter has been a testimony to the universal languages of wisdom and joy, accessible to all beings who open their hearts to listen.

Reflective questions:

- Can you think of a time when a moment of laughter or joy led to an unexpected insight or shift in perspective? What was the situation, and how did it change your view or approach to a particular aspect of your life?
- Do you remember an encounter with an animal or a moment in nature that brought you unexpected joy or laughter? How did this experience connect you to the larger web of life and its inherent wisdom?

As we transition from these stories to a more reflective space, I will share my practices for inviting the lighter side of spirit into my daily life.

Wisdom and Laughter: Playing Life Grand Games

Life, in its essence, is a grand game filled with opportunities for wisdom and bursts of laughter. Approaching our daily adventures with the spirit of playfulness allows us to navigate the world with a lighter heart and a joyful soul. Here are the playful practices that have become my strategies for embracing life's game:

Joyful Groove: Dance as Therapy:

Imagine your living room as your private dance floor, where your reflection cheers you on, free from judgment. I often lose myself in music, dancing to tunes that bring back happy memories or simply lift my spirit. In these moments, as I let joy lead the dance, laughter bubbles up, reminding me of the pure delight of existence. Dancing becomes not just a movement but a celebration of being alive.

Dancing has multiple benefits, from improving physical health by enhancing cardiovascular endurance, muscle strength, balance, and flexibility to boosting mental health by reducing symptoms of depression and anxiety. As a form of joyful exercise, dancing embodies these benefits, making my living room dance-offs not just fun but a holistic health practice.

Colorful Expressions: Releasing our Inner Artist:

I dedicate time to playing with colors and shapes, engaging in a silent dialogue with my inner child. This is not about creating masterpieces but about letting my soul's colors flow freely, finding joy and amusement in the unexpected patterns and stories that emerge. It is a reminder that life's canvas is vast and inviting, ready for us to make our mark with a spirit of exploration and fun.

Various studies have revealed that drawing brings a range of cognitive benefits. In particular, it enhances memory by demanding intricate visual processing. When I indulge in casual drawing, it is not exclusively about expressing myself; rather, it helps me see the world with more accuracy and originality, fortifying the link between playful art and cognitive well-being.

A Heartfelt Connection: Hug a Tree:

Among the playful practices that sprinkle laughter and wisdom into my daily life, embracing a tree holds a special place. There is something inherently grounding and uplifting about wrapping my arms around a tree, feeling its bark against my skin, and connecting with this living entity.

This simple connection has roots in various cultural practices and is supported by research, including insights from the Hug Doctor, who emphasizes the profound emotional and physiological benefits of hugging. Furthermore, the concept of biophilia highlights our innate connection to nature and its positive impact on our well-being.

Tree-hugging rituals can reduce stress, improve mood, and enhance immune system function. Engaging in this tender exchange with a tree reminds us of our interconnectedness with all living beings and the Earth. It is a physical manifestation of gratitude and reverence for the natural world, inviting laughter through its simplicity and profound peace in its execution. Next time you pass by a tree, I encourage you to pause, breathe with it, embrace it, and feel the shared life force that pulses through us all.

Laughter Therapy: Hasna Yoga:

My first incursion into laughter yoga was a big step outside my comfort zone, feeling somewhat awkward as I joined a circle of strangers ready to laugh without reason. Yet, as we began, something magical happened. The initial discomfort faded, replaced by genuine laughter and communal joy.

This practice, blending playful laughter exercises with the deep breaths of yoga, taught me a valuable lesson about embracing discomfort as a gateway to joy. It is a powerful reminder that sometimes, to find light-heartedness and connect deeply with others, we must be willing to step out of our comfort zones and into the game. In the unexpected and unfamiliar, it is here that laughter becomes not just an exercise but a celebration of breaking barriers and discovering new facets of our joy.

There are numerous health benefits of laughter, including the release of endorphins, the body's natural feel-good chemicals. Laughter yoga is more than an awkward first step into a circle of strangers; it is a scientifically supported method for improving mood, reducing stress, and even enhancing our immune system.

By stepping outside my comfort zone into laughter yoga, I am actively participating in a practice that is both ancient and validated by modern medicine as a way to enhance physical and mental well-being.

So, as we wrap up this chapter, let us carry forward the playful spirit that infuses our quest for wisdom. Let the stories and practices shared here inspire you to see life as a game filled with challenges but abundant with opportunities for joy, laughter, and light-hearted discovery.

As we leave behind the guardians of wisdom and laughter, carrying with us the light-hearted yet profound truths shared through joy and laughter, we prepare to step into the cyclical dance of nature and life. This journey has taught us that wisdom wears many faces and laughter serves as a key to unlocking the deepest of truths. Now, we pivot toward the eternal rhythms that govern all existence, ready to immerse ourselves in the profound cycles that shape our very being and the world around us.

CHAPTER V

CYCLES OF NATURE AND LIFE

"We are all just walking each other home."
– Ram Dass.

The tapestry of our lives is woven with the threads of nature's cycles, creating patterns of beauty, transformation, and continuity. This final chapter is an invitation to explore the ebb and flow of life's rhythms, to discover the wisdom embedded in the natural world, and to align ourselves with the universal dance of creation and dissolution.

Throughout my journey, I have experienced moments of profound connection with the natural cycles of life. These experiences have blurred the boundaries between myself and nature, revealing the intricate web of life that connects us all.

Whether I am surrounded by the majestic expanse of the Blue Mountains, where the endless cycle of seasons paints the landscape in countless shades of colors, participating in the magical celebrations of the Day of the Dead in Mexico, or practicing yoga on my mat, I have come to understand life itself as a mosaic of cycles.

This chapter explores how embracing the cycles of nature and life can lead to a deeper understanding of ourselves and our place in the cosmos. It is about finding peace in the knowledge that change is the only constant and that every ending is a prelude to a new beginning.

As we embark on this journey together, I encourage you to take a moment to contemplate the patterns that shape your days, the seasons of your heart, and the stages of your growth. Let us embrace the natural rhythms of life, not as obstacles to be overcome but as a beautiful dance that invites us to move with grace, resilience, and a deep sense of connection to the eternal becoming.

I hope that by sharing these stories and insights, you will find comfort in the cyclical nature of existence and appreciate the beauty of the transitions that shape our journey. May we all learn to dance in harmony with the cycles of nature and life, discovering the melody of our souls in their rhythm.

"Paradox of Existence"—*Australia*

At the outset of our adventures in Australia and New Zealand in 2023, I found myself venturing beyond the familiar landscapes of Sydney for the first time. My travels led me to the mystical Blue Mountains, a realm where the ancient spirits of nature—devas, gnomes, fairies, sylphs, undines, and salamanders—whispered the secrets of the Earth's ancient garden, Pangea. Here, amidst the sacred echoes of a bygone world, I found myself in a profound communion with elemental forces, witnessing their jubilant orchestration of the natural world's grand design.

Entering this enchanted forest, I felt enveloped by a symphony of harmonious energy, where the kingdoms of nature came together into a single, timeless present. The vibrant tapestry of green, woven by diverse flora and animated by the lively calls of cockatoos, crows, and kookaburras overhead, painted a scene of peaceful coexistence.

Beneath this aerial ballet, wallabies, kangaroos, and a host of other beings roamed freely, embodying the serene pulse of life.

The scent of different eucalyptus trees filled the air, softly enveloping my senses. Amidst this living mosaic, the towering eucalyptus trees stood as silent sentinels, shedding their bark in a ritual of renewal and growth. This act of natural shedding mirrored my own internal process of letting go, making space for new insights and personal evolution.

The forest's regenerative power in the aftermath of a fire, alongside the wise teachings of the fern trees, unfolded before me as a testament to nature's resilience and adaptability—echoing my journey of self-transformation.

VOICE OF THE PORTALS I: THE FIRST GATEWAY

With each step deeper into the canyons, I tread upon a living archive of the Earth's memory. The artistry of the wind and water on the sandstones reminded me of nature's endless cycle of creation and erosion, sculpting beauty from the raw fabric of existence. It was here, amidst these ancient formations, that I contemplated the essential role of everything in creation. The silent wisdom echoed, reminding me that profound insights exist everywhere. It also reminded me that the invisible could become visible if one knows how to look.

As I contemplated the teachings of the fern trees and the sculpting prowess of wind and water, I mused that the new earth unfolded like a tapestry woven with threads of intention, a realm of personal choice.

As I emerged from the forest, the landscape had transformed—or perhaps it was I who had changed. The world around me, once familiar, now appeared as a canvas of endless possibilities, reflecting the perpetual motion of life and nature's inherent change.

This journey through the Blue Mountains became more than a physical exploration; it was a pilgrimage into the heart of the interconnected tapestry of life, leading me toward an ever-evolving understanding of myself and my place within the natural world.

"Day of the Dead"—Mexico

In late October of 2023, my husband and I joined an international group of entrepreneurs to explore the vibrant heart of Oaxaca during the Day of the Dead celebrations. This journey, set against the backdrop of marigold-adorned altars and the rich scent of copal incense, became a profound exploration of life's fleeting nature and the rich tapestry of human connection.

The sound of ceremonial drums filled the narrow alleys, creating a rhythmic sensation that matched my own heartbeat. As I walked through the picturesque alleys, I was reminded of the fragility of life and felt the weight of my mortality. The flickering candlelight cast shadows on the cobblestone streets, reflecting the dance between life and death playing out in my soul.

As I walked through the bustling streets, I found myself surrounded by a diverse group of individuals who, at first glance, appeared to have very little in common. However, as we spent time together, I discovered that we all shared a profound understanding of our own mortality. Despite our differences, this realization brought us closer together, like kindred spirits. Moving through the highs and lows of life, we were aware that death is an inevitable part of this journey.

As we journeyed together, the landscape transformed into a breathtaking display of colors and emotions. Laughter and quiet reflection mingled in the air, accompanied by the lively tunes of bands and the joyful sounds of children. Amidst the vibrant chaos, I faced the remnants of my past, letting go of the parts of myself that no longer served my personal growth. It was a symbolic shedding of old skin, like the marigold petals that softly fell to the ground.

The fragrant essence of Oaxacan cuisine filled the air, tempting my senses with the rich aroma of mole and the sweet scent of sugar skulls. Each flavor served as a poignant reminder of the delicate balance between joy and sorrow, life, and death, which characterizes our existence.

We honored our loved ones who had passed away in a peaceful and solemn ceremony. The altar was lit by candles, which illuminated the faces of the departed and cast a warm glow on their photographs. As I stood amidst the beautiful marigolds, I felt a strong sense of connection with those who had gone before me, a feeling that transcended the boundaries of time.

The people I had just met shared their stories of love and loss, and we all felt a deep connection beyond mere familiarity. As we honored our loved ones together, we found comfort and resilience in each other's company. Our souls were laid bare, revealing a common humanity that bound us together.

As the night grew darker, everything started to blur. The flickering candlelight made me feel like I was surrounded by something otherworldly. I could sense a connection between the living and the departed as if the veil between worlds was thinning.

In the heart of Oaxaca, amidst a range of emotions and celebrations of life and death, I discovered a profound truth. By confronting my mortality, letting go of my personal stories, and honoring those who had passed away, I found a sense of freedom. The mystical experience of the Day of the Dead became a transformative journey for me, a rebirth, and a poignant reminder that life is impermanent, and we must cherish every moment.

"Final Savasana"—Asana Practice

Yoga has been a constant companion on my journey since 2012. However, only recently did the true essence of the final pose, savasana, unveil itself to me with profound clarity.

Amidst the familiar tranquility of my yoga practice, this realization emerged as another step in my physical routine and a gateway to a deeper understanding of existence and consciousness.

In the peaceful serenity of the yoga studio, this newfound perception of savasana transformed a habitual ritual into a sacred passage. As I reclined on my mat, the cool surface grounding me more profoundly than before, I closed my eyes. I willingly surrendered to the mystical realm that lies at the confluence of consciousness and the ethereal, a realm perhaps made more accessible through the years of my practice but only now fully embraced.

The soft strains of ambient music cradled the room, and I allowed myself to be carried away by the gentle undulations of the melody.

With each passing breath, I felt the weight of the physical world dissolve, much like the relinquishing grip of wakefulness during the transition into sleep.

My mat became a vessel sailing on the sea of tranquility, navigating the currents of inner stillness. In the cocoon of darkness, my senses heightened. The scent of sandalwood-infused air lingered, an olfactory anchor to the present moment.

The studio, a place of physical practice, expanded beyond its walls into the boundless spaces of my inner landscape, where I contemplated the parallels between the dream state and our conscious waking life.

This time, as I journeyed deeper into the observative state, I reflected on the nature of our dreams—how we surrender to the unconscious realms without a conscious bind. It struck me that in sleep, we embark on journeys unknown, traversing landscapes and dimensions painted by the subconscious mind. The question echoed softly in my thoughts: "Can we dream ourselves awake?"

In the canvas of my mind, active dreams unfurled like scrolls of forgotten tales. I became a traveler in the realms of dream time, navigating the landscapes of symbolism and emotion.

Like a whispered secret, the dream beckoned me to uncover the hidden truths beneath the surface of waking reality. Could these dreams be the threads weaving an intricate tapestry that connected the conscious, unconscious, and superconscious? The known and the mysterious?

The transition from dream to wakefulness, from sleep to awareness, echoed the broader journey from life to death. In this final savasana, I contemplated the enigma of our mortality, a journey shrouded in the veil of the unknown. Traditions and beliefs, like ancient maps, attempt to guide us through the labyrinth of the afterlife, offering pathways to understanding the incomprehensible.

Yet, as I lay here, I realized that the key to approaching this inevitable transition with grace lay not in clinging to the familiar but in embracing the mystery. The very fabric of our existence is woven with threads of uncertainty, and in the final moments, we must learn to dance with the unknown.

Could I leave this plane with peace, untethered from the constraints of biology, stories, and the illusions of reality? The answer, I sensed, lay in letting go. Just as sleep surrenders us to the unconscious currents of dream time and dreams themselves are transient echoes in the vast expanse of the mind, so could the final moments be a graceful surrender.

In the depths of the mystical experience, I practiced releasing my grip on the tangible and embracing the intangible.

VOICE OF THE PORTALS I: THE FIRST GATEWAY

I allowed the fear of the unknown to be my teacher and dissipate like morning mist, replaced by a serene acceptance that, much like the impermanence of dreams, life is a fleeting dance with the cosmos.

This final savasana became more than a pose; it was a profound meditation on life, death, and the spaces between. It brought into focus the impermanence of our existence and the beauty of surrendering to the journey with peace and acceptance. As the music and my inner contemplations quieted, I emerged from the pose with a sense of serenity and a deeper understanding of the dance between the tangible and intangible aspects of being.

This realization, born from my practice and crystallized in the tranquility of the yoga studio, marks a pivotal moment in my journey. It underscores the transformative power of yoga not just as a physical discipline but as a spiritual practice that guides us through life's mysteries with grace and poise.

Reflections and Practices: The Eternal Dance

Before we delve into reflections, let us take a moment to contemplate our encounters with the rhythms of life. In the Blue Mountains, the vast landscapes reminded us that our lives are filled with peaks and valleys, each moment of vulnerability coupled with the strength to continue.

In Oaxaca, amidst the vibrant celebration of the Day of the Dead, I was reminded of the thin veil between the worlds of the living and the dead. This celebration is a vibrant honoring of life, a reminder that death is not an end but a part of the cyclical nature of existence, urging us to embrace life's beauty and impermanence.

The tranquility of Final Savasana introduced us to the cycle of ending and beginning anew, teaching us to let go and find peace in surrender. It echoes nature's rhythm of birth, death, and rebirth.

These sacred cycles intertwine seamlessly with our daily lives, revealing themselves in the seasons of our existence and in the silence filled with meaning.

Acknowledging this sacredness transforms our view of the ordinary, making each moment an extraordinary opportunity for mindfulness and connection.

Reflective Questions:

- Can you recall a significant period of change in your life? How can you relate this personal season of change to a specific season or cycle in nature? What lessons did this period teach you about growth, transformation, or letting go?
- Do you have a ritual or practice that helps you align with the natural cycles, such as celebrating a change of season or observing the phases of the moon? How does this practice deepen your connection to nature and to your own cycle of personal growth?

- How has acknowledging the impermanence of life, as mirrored in the cycles of nature, influenced your perspective on living and being present in the moment? Can you identify a specific instance where this awareness brought you peace or clarity?

Embracing Nature's Cycles: Blending Daily Intentions with Personal Rituals

In my life, I do not just observe the natural cycles, but I also integrate them deeply through various practices that help me connect to the rhythm of existence. These rituals and spontaneous moments of connection serve as a bridge between the universe's macrocosm and my journey of growth and transformation.

Lunar Alchemy: Fire & Moon Ceremonies:

The moon, with its mysterious and ever-changing phases, serves as a beautiful reminder of life's constant flux and the cycles of renewal. By aligning my activities and reflections with the moon's cycles—from the new moon, symbolizing new beginnings, to the full moon, reflecting fulfillment and release—I create a rhythm that echoes the natural world's innate wisdom.

New Moon Intentions: With each new moon, I set aside time to set intentions for the coming cycle. This is a moment of quiet reflection and hopeful aspiration, where I write down my desires and goals in a journal. This practice is a way of planting seeds for what I wish to grow in my life.

Full Moon-Fire Ceremony: I prefer to conduct my rituals outdoors on full moon nights, basking in the moon's silvery glow. I prepare a small, controlled fire within a safe container, mindful of my surroundings and the sacredness of the act. Lighting the fire (or a candle), I set my intention to let go of what does not serve me anymore, writing it on paper as a symbol of what I wish to release.

Offering the paper to the fire, I observe the transformation of my written words into smoke and ashes—a visual and symbolic release of outdated beliefs, thoughts, and energies. Watching the flames, I envision the moon's energy enveloping me, its light filling the voids within with newfound clarity, peace, and potential.

I conclude my ceremony in gratitude, honoring the fire, the moon, and the earth for their endless guidance and support. This ritual is a meditation on the cycle of destruction and rebirth that frames our existence, mirrored in the moon's phases and the fire's transformative power.

The transformative power of fire ceremonies is recognized in spiritual communities and psychological practices as a form of ritual therapy. Research into the psychological effects of ritualistic practices suggests that engaging in rituals can significantly reduce anxiety and increase feelings of control and efficacy.

Throughout history, various cultures have used fire in their ceremonies for environmental and personal purification. For instance, the Vedic traditions of India performed Agni Hotra, while indigenous cultures in the Americas also utilized fire to establish a divine connection and send prayers skyward. Additionally, many ancient civilizations, such as the Celts and Mayans, relied on the observation of lunar cycles to maintain cosmic harmony and balance in their calendars, agriculture, and spiritual rituals.

This blend of lunar observation and fire ritual is more than a personal practice; it is a living bridge to the collective wisdom of ages past, a reminder of the shared human journey through cycles of change and renewal.

Sacred Space: Altar Creation:

I have dedicated a special space in my home to honor loved ones, for contemplation, to focus on an intention, or to acknowledge personal milestones.

This altar serves as an anchor, a daily reminder of the cycle of life and death, keeping me connected to the wisdom and love of those who have touched my life. It is a tangible way to honor my journey and the lessons learned, enriching my path with a visible expression of my intentions and purpose.

Creating spaces for remembrance and honor has roots in many cultures and spiritual traditions around the world. It is a physical manifestation of our inner landscapes, a bridge between the material and spiritual worlds.

Historical evidence shows that altars have been used as sacred spaces for meditation, prayer, and communication with the divine across different civilizations, reflecting the human need for grounding and connection. In modern psychological practice, creating a space for honor and remembrance can aid in grieving, providing a tangible way to process loss and celebrate life.

The Gateway to Living Fully: Mindfulness of Death:

Perhaps the most profound practice I have integrated is contemplating my mortality. This reflection is not about dwelling on the end but enriching the journey. It reminds me to live with intention, savoring the beauty of each moment and embracing the transformation that each cycle of life brings.

By acknowledging life's impermanence, I have put my priorities and affairs in order, I feel connected to all but attached to nothing, and I find a deeper appreciation for the richer engagement with the cycles of nature, and a more heartfelt connection to others.

The Buddhist practice of Maranasati, or mindfulness of death, is a profound tool for embracing life's impermanence, leading to a more intentional and fulfilling existence. Contemporary research echoes this, suggesting that awareness of mortality can significantly impact our life choices and priorities, leading to a richer, more authentic life experience.

Simply Grateful: Gratitude Practice:

Each morning and evening, I take a moment to reflect on and write what I am thankful for. This simple act shifts my focus from lacking to the abundance surrounding me. It grounds me in the present and opens my heart to each new day's possibilities.

Cultivating gratitude has become a cornerstone of my daily life, infusing each moment with a sense of appreciation and contentment.

The benefits of gratitude have been extensively studied in positive psychology, with research showing that regular gratitude practices can enhance well-being, increase resilience, and improve relationships. A study found that people who regularly practiced gratitude felt better about their lives, experienced greater positive emotions, and were more optimistic about the future. Gratitude practices help us recognize the different ways of abundance in our lives, shifting our focus from scarcity to abundance.

In blending these practices into my daily life, I have discovered a richer, more nuanced understanding of nature's cycles and my journey through them.

I hope that by sharing these personal reflections and rituals, you, too, will be inspired to see the sacred rhythms of nature reflected in your path, finding beauty and wisdom in the eternal dance of life. Let us carry this awareness with us, finding in each breath a connection to the infinite cycle of being and, in each moment, an opportunity to be fully present in the wondrous journey of life.

As we prepare to turn the final pages of our journey together in "Voice of the Portals I: The First Gateway," it is a moment to pause and reflect on the path we have traversed. From the sacred echoes of ancient landscapes to the intimate dance of our inner transformations, this expedition has been more than a collection of stories and practices—it has been an invitation to see the world and ourselves through a lens of wonder and interconnectedness.

We have shared moments of deep reflection, laughter, and discovery, each step guided by the rhythms of nature and the whispers of our souls.

As we stand at the threshold of what feels like an end, remember that it is merely a gateway to new beginnings. The insights and experiences we have gathered here are seeds for the journey ahead, ready to blossom in the soil of our continued quest for understanding and connection.

EPILOGUE

BEYOND THE FIRST GATEWAY

As we close the pages of "Voice of the Portals I: The First Gateway," I pause, reflecting not just on the journeys inked across these pages but also on the paths that lie uncharted before us. This book, a tapestry woven from the ancient whispers of the earth and the silent songs of the stars, stands as a beacon for the boundless mysteries that surround us and reside within us. It is a narrative that has invited us to explore not only the physical marvels of our planet but also the profound depths of our inner landscapes.

This epilogue is not an end but a threshold, beckoning us toward further exploration, deeper understanding, and even more transformative adventures. It marks a pivotal moment where we acknowledge the power of endings as gateways to new beginnings, each step an integral part of an ongoing journey.

In an age where digital screens often eclipse the stars, our shared narrative serves as a reminder of the enduring power of storytelling. It is a call to weave our tales with intention and to live each day as if it were a page in an epic saga where we are both the authors and the heroes.

Through our journey, we have encountered landscapes that challenged us, wisdom that changed us, and laughter that bonded us, highlighting the rich tapestry of shared human experience.

As we peer into the horizon, new adventures whisper their invitations. The lands yet to be explored call out, promising tales of wonder and insights yet to be uncovered.

"Voice of the Portals II: The Second Journey" awaits, promising to be a continuum of our shared pilgrimage—one that I hope you will join me on.

This journey extends beyond mere exploration; it is an invitation to forge a deeper bond with our world. It is a quest to discover the strength in stillness, the wisdom in whispers, and the connections that exist not within the confines of technology but in the unspoken unity of the universe.

As we step beyond the first gateway, let us embrace the teachings of the natural world. Let us carry forward the stories heard in the rustling leaves and the murmuring streams, and let these experiences remind us to approach life with eyes wide with wonder and hearts open to understanding.

In parting, I invite you, my fellow travelers, to continue this journey with me, to explore the endless possibilities that await. Together, let us vow to reclaim the stories of our lives, to infuse our days with the magic of discovery, and to celebrate the countless ways we are intertwined with the mysteries of this magnificent planet.

Until our paths cross again in the next chapter of our quest, may your way be filled with curiosity, your spirit with bravery, and your story with moments that echo through time.

The journey is far from over; it is merely stretching its wings for the next flight. I look forward to sharing it with you, embracing both the profound and the sacred.

Farewell for now. We will gather once more at the next gateway, ready to delve deeper into the mysteries that unite us.

ACKNOWLEDGMENTS

Reflecting on the journey of bringing "Voice of the Portals" to life, I am filled with profound gratitude for the myriad of support, inspiration, and guidance I have received. This book is not just a product of my solitary musings, but a tapestry woven from the contributions of many incredible individuals and sources of inspiration.

The natural world deserves my first and most heartfelt acknowledgment. The landscapes that whisper secrets, the winds that guide, the waters that soothe, the animals and the stones that endure have been my most profound teachers. They've spoken in the silent language of the soul, guiding my steps on this path of discovery and connection.

As I embark on this narrative journey, it is with deep respect and acknowledgment that I also recognize the First Nations, the original custodians of the lands and waters from which the inspirations for "Voice of the Portals" have sprung. Their profound connection to the earth, enduring wisdom, and stewardship of the sacred landscapes are the foundation upon which this work rests. I offer my sincere gratitude for their direct and observed teachings and for the cultural, spiritual, and physical connections they maintain with Mother Earth. It is upon their unceded territories that many of the sacred sites mentioned in this book are located, and I extend my respect to their elders, past, present, and future.

I am eternally grateful to my husband, Henry, my daughter Ayana, and my family and friends, whose unwavering support and love have been my anchor in times of doubt and my sail in moments of inspiration. Your belief in me has been a source of strength that has propelled me forward, even when the path seemed unclear.

A special Thank you to Malieokalani Urrutia, one of my mentors and teachers, whose encouragement and guidance have been instrumental in this endeavor. Your support in sharing these stories and your role as a catalyst guiding me to integrate my experiences into coherent narratives has been priceless. Your platform has allowed my tales to take flight; I am grateful for that.

I am deeply grateful to all my spiritual guides and mentors, both seen and unseen, who have illuminated my path with their wisdom and insight. Your teachings have been a beacon of light, guiding me toward a deeper understanding of myself, the universe, and my place within it.

ACKNOWLEDGMENTS

To you, my fellow travelers and readers, who are embarking on this journey with me. Your curiosity, openness, and thirst for knowledge inspire me. This book was crafted to rekindle the light of exploration and wonder within you.

To the artists, dreamers, and visionaries whose work has inspired me, your ability to capture the essence of the ethereal and the tangible has been a wellspring of inspiration. Your creativity ignites the imagination and opens the heart to the beauty surrounding us.

ChatGPT, my digital assistant, deserves mention for its role in this creative process. Its assistance in refining my thoughts, expanding my ideas, and sometimes simply being a sounding board has been invaluable. This collaboration between humans and artificial intelligence is a testament to our incredible era, where technology and spirituality can intersect in fascinating ways.

I extend my heartfelt appreciation to Katherine Adegoke of Katherine Editorials for her invaluable expertise and unwavering dedication as the editor of this book. Your insightful contributions have truly enhanced the quality and clarity of the content.

Finally, to the sacred sites, portals, and thresholds that have called to me across time and space, thank you for your silent wisdom and the lessons you have imparted. You are the true authors of these stories, and I am but a scribe who has attempted to translate your timeless wisdom into words.

May this book be a gateway for others as it has been for me, leading to new horizons of understanding, compassion, and connection.

Here is to the journey that continues beyond the final page into the great unknown with an open heart and an eager spirit.

With deepest gratitude and love,
Hellevi E. Woodman.

JOURNEY TO THE HEART

In the silence between worlds,
Whispers of the ancient earth speak,
Guiding us through portals unseen,
To the sacred heart of the mystical deep.
Beneath the canopy of cosmic dance,
Where shadows merge with light,
Our spirits soar on wings of chance,
Towards the essence of our might.
Through the gateways of the soul,
Past the veils of time and space,
We journey to become whole,
In the embrace of the earth's grace.
With each step on this sacred ground,
Our hearts awaken to the call,
In the depth of connection found,
We discover we are part of it all.
So let us walk with reverence,

On this path of ancient lore,
Embracing the presence,
Of the wisdom that came before.
For, in the end, our journey's plea,
Is to return to the heart's knowing,
That we are one with the mystery,
In the endless cycle of becoming.

GLOSSARY OF TERMS

1. *Consciousness*: The state of being aware of and able to think, feel, and experience oneself and the environment.
2. *Energy:* The invisible force that flows through all things, connecting life and matter in the universe.
3. *Intuition*: The ability to instinctively understand something without conscious reasoning.
4. *Mindfulness*: Maintaining a non-judgmental state of heightened or complete awareness of one's thoughts, emotions, or experiences on a moment-to-moment basis.
5. *Portal:* A gateway to another dimension or state of consciousness, often found in sacred or energetically charged locations.
6. *Sacred Sites*: Places of spiritual significance, revered for their historical, natural, or cultural energies that connect the physical and spiritual realms.

7. *Shamanism*: an ancient healing tradition based on the belief in an interconnected universe, where the shaman acts as an intermediary between the physical and spiritual worlds.

8. *Earthing*: connecting physically to the earth to balance the body's energies, often by walking barefoot, to improve health and well-being.

9. *Dreamtime:* A foundational concept in Aboriginal Australian cultures, Dreamtime refers to the ancestral period of creation when the spiritual, natural, and moral elements of the universe were established. It encompasses the stories and ceremonies that describe the journeys of ancestral beings as they created the landscapes, plants, animals, and customs that inhabit the Earth.

10. *Synchronicity*: The occurrence of events that appear significantly related but have no discernible causal connection, often perceived as meaningful coincidences within spiritual journeys.

11. *Ancestral Wisdom*: Knowledge and teachings passed down through generations, emphasizing the importance of heritage and tradition in understanding and navigating life.

12. *Eco Spirituality*: A belief system that recognizes the sacredness of all nature and emphasizes the interconnectedness of humans with the Earth and its ecosystems.

13. *Vibration*: The frequency at which energy in various forms, including thoughts, sound, and light, vibrates. It is often used in spiritual contexts to describe the energy state of beings and objects.

FURTHER READINGS

In "The Voice of Portals," we traverse a landscape rich with mystical insights and spiritual awakenings. For those readers inspired to delve deeper into the themes explored within its pages, the following list of further readings offers a gateway to a broader understanding of sacred sites, spirituality, mindfulness, ancient wisdom, and the interconnectedness of all life.

These books are selected to complement the journey you have embarked on and to guide you further along your path of exploration and discovery.

1. *"The Power of Now" by Eckhart Tolle*—A guide to spiritual enlightenment that emphasizes the importance of living in the present moment and transcending thoughts and ego.

2. *"Secrets of Meditation: A Practical Guide to Inner Peace and Personal Transformation" by Davidji*—This book offers a deep dive into meditation and guides readers on a journey to inner peace and personal transformation through mindfulness and awareness.

3. *"Conscious Dreaming: A Spiritual Path for Everyday Life" by Robert Moss*—A comprehensive guide to understanding dreams and using them for personal growth and exploration.

4. *"The Divine Blueprint: Temples, Power Places, and the Global Plan to Shape the Human Soul" by Freddy Silva*—An insightful exploration into the secret codes and spiritual significance of ancient and modern sacred sites worldwide.

5. *"Peace Is Every Step: The Path of Mindfulness in Everyday Life" by Thich Nhat Hanh*—A beautiful introduction to mindfulness practice and finding joy in peaceful living by one of the most revered Zen masters in the world.

6. *"The Book of Secrets: Unlocking the Hidden Dimensions of Your Life" by Deepak Chopra*—Chopra explores the mysteries of life from a spiritual perspective, offering insights into finding harmony and deeper meaning.

7. *"Wherever You Go, There You Are" by Jon Kabat-Zinn*—This book introduces mindfulness meditation as a practice and a way of being accessible to all.

8. *"The Inside-Out Revolution" by Michael Neill*—This book offers practical guidance for anyone looking to transform their life by shifting their perspective, making it essential for psychological and spiritual growth.

9. *"Laughter Therapy: How to Laugh About Everything in Your Life That Isn't Really Funny" by Annette Goodheart*—This book offers insights into using laughter as a therapeutic tool to deal with life's challenges. It emphasizes how laughter can transform our perspective and bring healing to emotional and physical ailments.

10. *"Walking Each Other Home: Conversations on Loving and Dying" by Ram Dass and Mirabai Bush*—This book explores the spiritual dimensions of death and dying, offering insights into how love can guide us through life's ultimate journey. It resonates with the theme of conscious living and dying.

11. *"The Power of Myth—Embarking on a Mystical Journey" by Joseph Campbell* explores myth's enduring power in understanding life's deeper meanings and the human journey.

12. *"The Field: The Quest for the Secret Force of the Universe" by Lynne McTaggart*—A fascinating look into the science of the interconnectedness of all things and the power of our thoughts and intentions.

13. *"The Heart of the Shaman: Stories and Practices of the Luminous Warrior" by Alberto Villoldo*—The book delves into shamanic practices and teachings for healing and creating a life filled with spiritual connection and purpose.

ABOUT ME

From the vibrant spotlight of a cruise ship stage to the serene expanses of nature's most sacred spaces, my path has been anything but linear.

I am Hellevi, a Venezuelan-American artist with over three decades of experience in the performing arts, a rich history as a dancer and illusionist, and more than ten years as an entertainer on cruise ships. These extraordinary adventures of my life allowed me to immerse myself in our planet's vibrant cultures and breathtaking landscapes, enriching my soul and expanding my understanding of the world.

My journey has been richly adorned with experiences as a mindful nature guide and practitioner of active dreaming, taking me through transformative personal milestones enriched by yoga, meditation, and holistic wellness. A pivotal moment in 2012 led to a profound spiritual awakening in 2019, further deepened by the study and practice of shamanic traditions.

As a holistic health coach, yoga teacher, and Reiki master, and without adherence to any specific spiritual framework, my path is one of heartful living, embracing the wisdom of the earth and the universe in its myriad forms. My understanding of age-old wisdom, mastery of breathwork, expertise in sound therapy, and my roles as a ceremonial leader and a compassionate psychedelic-assisted end-of-life doula reflect my commitment to exploring the mystical aspects of existence.

I am deeply passionate about uncovering the spiritual, not confined by the boundaries of traditional beliefs and disciplines, utilizing sacred, practical tools for conscious existence, dreaming, and navigating life's transitions.

My work and writings are a testament to a life dedicated to exploring the depths of the human spirit and the interconnectedness of all life, aiming to guide others on their path to self-discovery and holistic well-being.

Connect with me on:

- Hellevi E. Woodman
- hellevi.ew

www.ingramcontent.com/pod-product-compliance
Lightning Source LLC
LaVergne TN
LVHW051131080426
835510LV00018B/2345